WOW!

Exploring God's World of Wonder with Preschoolers

Group

Loveland, Colorado

W*O*W! Exploring God's World of Wonder With Preschoolers

Credits

Contributing Authors: Delphine Boswell, Joy B. Cole, Mary Ann Craven, Debbie Gowensmith, Karen B. Humphrey, Julie Lavender, Carol Mader, Bonnie Temple, and Dave Thornton

Book Acquisitions Editor: Beth Rowland
Editor: Debbie Gowensmith
Quality Control Editor: Jennifer Root Wilger
Chief Creative Officer: Joani Schultz
Copy Editor: Shirley Michaels
Art Director: Ragont Design
Illustrators: Bron Smith, Mary Ragont
Computer Graphic Artist: Ragont Design
Cover Art Director: Jeff A. Storm
Cover Designer: Color Forms Art Studio
Cover Illustrator: Bryan Bandyk
Production Manager: Peggy Naylor

Library of Congress Cataloging-in-Publication Data
W*O*W: exploring God's world of wonder with preschoolers.
     p. cm.
    Includes indexes.
    ISBN 0-7644-2107-7 (alk. paper)
    1. Creation 2. Nature—Religious aspects—Christianity. 3. Christian education of preschool children. I. Group Publishing.
    II. Title: WOW!
    BT695.5.W2 1999
    268'.432—dc21
                                                        98-31884
                                                            CIP

10 9 8 7 6 5 4 3 2 1   08 07 06 05 04 03 02 01 00 99
Printed in the United States of America.

Contents

Introduction

Preschoolers are fascinated by the natural world. They're amused by roly-poly bugs that tightly curl and by elephants that swing long trunks back and forth. They're enthralled with fuzzy caterpillars, tall giraffes, squooshy mud, speckled rocks, twinkling stars, gentle rain, and warm sand.

Preschoolers are energetic and enthusiastic explorers, too. Young children fill their days with watching, touching, listening, smelling, and tasting their world. Sometimes their explorations yield delightful results—the softness of a flower's fragrant petals—and sometimes they yield disastrous results—the musty smell and gritty texture of dirt. But young children continue exploring with exuberant spirits and wondering minds.

As children explore, they develop theories about how the world works— the ideas and beliefs that often stay with them throughout their lives, even if those ideas aren't accurate and even if later education attempts to correct them (Howard Gardner, *The Unschooled Mind*). So what we teach preschoolers is incredibly important. We can help children see—for the rest of their lives— that God is a wonderful, intelligent, loving creator.

The lessons in *W*O*W! Exploring God's World of Wonder With Preschoolers* connect children's discoveries about the world to their Creator. Every activity teaches young children something awesome about God and his creation. When children discover that blue and yellow make green, they'll praise God for creating colors. When children splash in cool water, they'll thank God for the gift of water.

Each lesson includes three segments:

● "God Created ...": In three activities, children will explore what God created. For example, in "God Created Cold," children will play with ice, paint with ice cubes, and discover ways to cool things that are warm.

● "... Is in the Bible": In three activities, children will learn what the Bible says about creation. For example, in "Dirt and Rocks Are in the Bible," children will create sculptures from dirt, add sound effects to the story of the man who built a house on rock, and hear about the good dirt in which plants grow.

● "Let's Thank God for ...": In one activity, children will thank God for his creation. For example, in "Let's Thank God for Seasons," children will create motions to represent the seasons and then perform them during a prayer.

Through the lessons in this book, children can learn that not only the heavens "declare the glory of God" (Psalm 19:1), but also the oceans and the weather and the seasons and even the dirt under our feet. Enjoy exploring God's world with the preschoolers you teach!

God Created Cold

Cold cheeks and red noses, ice cream and swimming pools, the wind and rain—these are cold things God made for us to enjoy. The cold God created balances the heat and encourages the world to rest. Cold things replenish and rejuvenate us.

Preschoolers love cold things and experience them in everyday life—ice, puddles, Popsicles, and puppy dog noses, for example. When we help young children identify, describe, and explain what they're experiencing, we help them to more deeply explore and understand God's delightful world. Use this lesson to help children playfully discover that God made the cold for us to enjoy and that cold is good.

Supply List

- a Bible
- a large bag of ice cubes
- a dishpan-sized plastic tub
- hand towels or paper towels
- an assortment of gloves and mittens, such as rubber gloves, wool mittens or gloves, and cooking mitts (one glove or mitten per child)
- newsprint
- paint smocks or old T-shirts
- different colors of tempera paint
- water
- liquid soap
- a spoon
- ice-cube trays
- one sheet of white butcher paper or construction paper for each child

- a fan
- warm water
- a cake pan (9x13)
- bananas, one or two for every six children
- a knife
- assorted frozen fruit, such as peach or strawberry slices
- milk
- a blender
- small cups
- a pan of white tempera paint
- a large paintbrush
- dark blue or black construction paper
- glue
- cotton balls
- an iron
- an ice chest to store all frozen items

Preparation

Dilute different colors of tempera paint with a little water. Add a small amount of liquid soap to the paint, and stir gently to avoid creating bubbles. Fill the ice-cube trays with tempera paint, and put them in the freezer.

Freeze the bananas in their peels. Just before class, peel the bananas, and cut them in half.

God Created Cold

1. Let's Explore

Put about one-third of the ice cubes in the plastic tub and set it in the center of a table. Also set out the mittens and gloves. Then gather the children around the table.

Stir the ice with your bare hand and say: **Brr! These ice cubes are cold! Put your hand in here and touch the ice. Why do you think God made ice so cold?** Give children time to touch the ice cubes and respond.

Say: **Cold things cool us off and make us feel good. These ice cubes can make drinks cold, or they can make us cold if we hold them in our hands.**

Have children dry off their hands. Say: **Let's try an experiment. An experiment is what scientists do when they're learning about something. Let's be scientists today and learn about cold. Put one of these gloves or mittens on one of your hands.**

Help children put on the gloves and mittens, and then say: **I'm going to put an ice cube in your hands. Hold the ice cube with each hand, and then tell me which hand feels colder: your bare hand or your gloved hand.** Give each child an ice cube, and ask:

● **Which hand feels colder? warmer? Why?**
● **When do cold things like ice feel good? bad?**

Have the children put the ice cubes back into the tub, and then say: **You are all such good scientists! The mitten protects your hand from cold. God made the cold. He didn't want us to get too hot. He wanted the world to be a happy place for us to live. We need both hot and cold. Let's try another experiment now.**

Add some fresh ice to the tub, and then set it on the floor. Say: **Here's a lot of ice. God covered some places in the world with lots of great big pieces of ice called icebergs. Polar bears and penguins live where there are lots of icebergs. Can we live on the ice like polar bears and penguins can?** Allow children to respond. **No, it would be too cold for us,** wouldn't it? But a little ice and cold is good. Ask:

● **What happens to ice when we put something warm, like our hands, on it?**

Say: **When we put something warm on ice, it starts to melt. Let's see if we can melt a bit of this ice using our warm bodies. If the ice starts to feel uncomfortable on your skin, touch the ice to a different place on your body.**

Have children work together—using hands, arms, elbows, and legs—to make the ice melt. After a few minutes, dry everyone off, and ask:

● **Which parts of your body felt the coldest?**

● **Why did God make cold things for us?**

Say: **God made the cold. I'm glad for cold things, aren't you?**

Discard the ice from the tub.

2. Ice Cube Paintings

Have children put on paint smocks or old T-shirts for this activity. Cover a table with newsprint. Set the ice cube paints in the plastic tub, and put it in the center of the table. Have children gather around the table, and give each child a piece of white paper.

Say: **Let's make some icy pictures to remind us that God made the cold!** Show children how to rub the ice cubes on their papers to paint pictures. As preschoolers work, encourage them to try different ways to use their paints. For example, children can breathe on the cubes, causing them to melt, and then draw with them. Or children can set their cubes on their papers, causing the cubes to melt and leave a print, while they warm their hands. Or children can make hand prints as the cubes melt onto their hands. Accept and praise the different ways the preschoolers paint.

Teacher Tip

During a cold season, end this activity by having children warm their hands in a pan of warm water or put their dry hands on a warm heating pad. Tell children that God made both hot and cold so we could be happy.

Teacher Tip

Use a warm iron to heat the pieces of paper right before children begin painting.

Teacher Tip

During a warm season, have children paint outside. The paint cubes will melt faster when children put their papers on a warm sidewalk.

Teacher Tip

Don't use uncomfortably hot water in case children touch the pan or the water.

As children finish their drawings, say: **You are such good scientists and artists! You painted beautiful pictures with your paint cubes. I'm glad God made the cold! It makes our world a fun place to live in!**

Either discard the remaining paint cubes, or return them to the ice trays to refreeze them. Have children take off their smocks; wipe or rinse out the plastic tub.

3. We Can Make Things Cold

Put warm water into the cake pan. Place the pan and the fan near you.

Gather children around you. Jump up and down, and say: **I'm exercising so much, and I'm getting really hot! Jump with me!** After a few jumps, ask:

● **Are you getting hot?**

● **What could we do to cool off?**

Keep jumping up and down until children tell you to stop jumping or mention other ways to cool off. Then turn on the fan, and sit near it with the children so it blows on everyone. Say: **That's better! When we stop jumping, we cool off. The wind from the fan also cools us off. The wind God made helps to keep us cool.**

Show children the pan of warm water, and say: **Here's something else that's hot. If we wanted to drink this water or take a bath in it and if it were too hot, how could we make it cooler?** Give children time to respond. Then use a child's idea to cool the water—blow on it together or add cold water or ice, for example. Then ask:

● **What things did God give us to make things cold?**

● **How do you best like to cool off when you're too hot?**

Say: **God loves you and made ways to cool off so you wouldn't get too hot! Let's play a game to thank God for making the cold. I'm going to name some words. If I name something warm or hot, droop to the floor as though you're an ice cube that's melting. Let's try melting like an ice cube.** Wait for children to respond, and then say: **Good job! If I name something cold, jump up with your hands in the air and say, "Thank you, God, for the cold."** Let's try that. Say: **Ice cube**, and lead children in jumping with raised hands and saying, "Thank you, God, for the cold." Say: **I think you're ready to play the game! Listen carefully to each word, and decide if I'm naming something hot or cold.**

Say several words—ice cream, hot bath, sunshine, snow, swimming pool, hot chocolate, heating pad, blankets, rain, winter coats, bathing suits, a dog's wet nose, a winter day, a hug, a pet—and allow children to respond to each word.

Cold Is in the Bible

1. A Cold Drink

Open the Bible to Proverbs 25:25 (New Century Version). Show children the page, and say: **Proverbs 25:25 in the Bible talks about how good cold water feels. It says, "Good news from a faraway place is like a cool drink when you are tired." This means that getting a letter or a phone call from someone we love who lives far away is as nice as a cold drink of water when we're thirsty. Are any of you thirsty?**

After children have responded, say: **God gave us cold things to drink when we're thirsty, so let's make some special cold drinks. You can help me.** Set out the bag of clean ice cubes, the frozen bananas, the assorted frozen fruit, and the milk.

Have children take turns helping you put three or four ice cubes, two or three banana halves, a large spoonful of assorted frozen fruit, and some milk into a blender. Blend the mixture, adding extra milk or bananas to give it the consistency of a milkshake. When you have finished mixing one batch, pour the drink into cups, and have children serve one another. Make enough for every child to have some.

Say: **Mmm, that hit the spot! I'm glad God gave us cold things to drink! We made a great snack today by putting all these cold things together! You were good helpers.**

Have children throw away their cups.

2. A Cold-and-Hot Promise Path

Put a piece of newsprint, about six to eight feet long, on the floor. Add more ice to the plastic dish tub, and place it at one end of the newsprint path. Fill the cake pan with warm water again, and place it at the other end of the newsprint path. Place towels next to the cake pan.

Have the children sit on the floor near you. Open a Bible to Genesis 8:22. Show them the Bible, and say: **God loves us so much that he made the cold and heat. He wants us to be safe and happy. Did you know that God has a promise for us in the Bible about heat and cold? Listen to what the Bible says.**

Read aloud Genesis 8:22: **"As long as the earth endures, seedtime and harvest, cold and heat, summer and winter, day and night will never cease." God says we will always have cold and heat, summer and winter, and day and night. God promises that we will always have hot and cold to keep us safe and comfortable. God promises these things because he loves us.**

Because God is faithful, he always keeps his promises. Can you say

Teacher Tip

Be sure to stand near the cake pan of warm water to help children step in and out without sliding.

"faithful" with me? Lead children in saying: **Faithful.** Then continue: **That's right. Let's do something fun to help us remember that God is faithful. God promises that we will always have cold and heat to enjoy.**

Have children take off their shoes and socks. Say: **We're going to take turns putting our feet in this ice. Then we're going to walk across the path all the way to the warm water, where we'll warm up our feet! When you put your feet in the warm water, smile and say, "Aah, God is faithful!"** Help children walk the path until everyone has had a turn.

After children have dried their feet, have them put their shoes and socks on. As they do, throw away the paper, and wipe up any wet spots on the floor. Then ask:

● **How did it feel to walk on cold ice and in warm water?**
● **Why do you think God gave us hot and cold?**

Say: **God loves us so much that he promises to always give us heat and cold. God is faithful, so he always keeps his promises. He'll always take care of us.**

3. A Chilly Picture

Put a few layers of newsprint on the floor. Nearby, place a pan of white tempera paint and a large paintbrush. Set dark construction paper, cotton balls, and glue in the center of a table.

Read Proverbs 25:13a to the children: **"Like the coolness of snow at harvest time is a trustworthy messenger to those who send him."**

Say: **Harvest time is when people pick all the food like fruits and vegetables they've been growing in their gardens. Cold snow at harvest time is a good thing. The cold makes the ground rest so it will be ready to grow food later. This Bible verse tells us that cold is a good thing. How many of you like snow? Do you wish you could play in the snow right now?** Allow children to respond. **Since we don't have snow in our classroom, let's make a snow picture with pretend snow. Our pictures can remind us that God made the cold and that it's good.**

Have children put on smocks or T-shirts again. Give each child a sheet of construction paper. Help children each glue cotton balls to a sheet of paper to make a snowman. Then have children tear small pieces of black construction paper scraps to glue on for eyes.

As children finish their snowmen, have them take turns placing their pictures on the newsprint on the floor. Dip the paintbrush into the white paint, and have each child stand over his or her picture. Help the child gently drip the white paint onto the picture. When the child is satisfied with the amount of "snow," set the picture aside to dry. Allow each child to drip snow on the picture.

As children work, say: **Remember, God made the cold, and it's good! You're doing a great job on your chilly pictures!**

When children are finished, have them clean their hands and take off their smocks. Say: **We had fun today exploring the cold God made. Now let's thank God for making the cold.**

Let's Thank God for Cold

1. Icy Prayers

Have children stand in a circle and put their hands behind their backs.
Say: **We've had fun today learning that God made the cold.** Ask:
● **What are some cold things God made for us?**

After children respond, say: **Those are special things God made. Let's**

Teacher Tip

You may want to ask an adult to help at the art table while you help children splatter paint on their pictures one at a time.

thank him now for making those things. I'm going to walk behind you. When I place an ice cube in your hand, thank God for something cold.

Walk behind the children, and put an ice cube in someone's hands. Have that child thank God for something cold. If children need help, suggest that they say, "Thank you, God, for ice cream" or "Thank you, God, for swimming pools" or "Thank you, God, for making the cold."

Randomly hand the ice cube to children until everyone has had a chance to pray. Then pray: **God, thank you for loving us so much that you thought of making cold things for us to enjoy. Thank you for your love. Amen.**

God Created Colors

Look around. Splashes of color from every direction meet your eye. God's palette is infinite; he is "the originator of colors and all their possible combinations" (Mark Twain, *Autobiography,* quoted in *The Book of Wisdom*). The imaginative and unreproducible colors in flowers, the sky, bird feathers, and even fish scales direct us toward a creative and loving God. He made a world in which colors attract, beautify, and add interest and fun!

Children of all ages love colors. But colors fascinate preschoolers, who are just learning to discover and identify colors. This lesson allows preschoolers to mix and separate colors, look "through" colors, create colors, and even imagine what colors God saw as he surveyed his new creation. Through these experiences, preschoolers can learn that our creative God loves them so much that he "paints" the world with interesting colors. Hop aboard the Rainbow Express; our next stop is the Land of Color!

Supply List

- an easy-to-understand Bible translation
- newspaper
- red, yellow, and blue food coloring
- clear plastic cups
- water
- several small cups or a white plastic ice-cube tray for each child
- straws
- a shallow saucer or bowl for each child
- paper towels
- green, orange, brown, purple, and black water-based markers
- a pitcher of water
- two-inch squares of construction paper in red, yellow, blue, green, orange, purple, brown, black, and white
- nature books with pictures of animals (optional)
- a variety of sliced fresh, defrosted, or canned fruit—for example, blueberries, raspberries, kiwis, bananas, peaches, oranges, and apples
- graham crackers
- cream cheese
- plastic knives
- paper plates
- one cardboard toilet paper tube for each child
- four-inch squares of red, yellow, and blue cellophane paper
- rubber bands

Teacher Tip

The rubber bands should be small enough to go around a toilet paper roll one time. Larger bands are difficult for children to handle.

13

Preparation

Fill four clear plastic cups with water. Use the food coloring to make red, yellow, and blue water. You'll need enough cups of water so they're easily accessible to all the children. Put a straw in each cup.

Try the "Separating Colors" experiment before class to determine which colors of markers to use. Depending on the brand of markers, different colors separate better than others.

Use the two-inch squares of construction paper to create a stack for each child. Each stack should contain these colors: red, yellow, blue, green, orange, purple, brown, black, and white.

God Created Colors

1. Name That Color

Cover a table with newspaper. Then set out the cups of food coloring and the cups or ice-cube trays. Also set out four extra clear plastic cups.

Have children gather around you, and say: **Today we're going to learn about the colors God made. What are some of your very favorite colors?** Allow children to respond. **God made lots of pretty colors because they're fun and help us to see things better.** Point out a child who's wearing brightly colored clothing. **I can see you better today because you're wearing such bright colors.**

God created so many pretty colors! But did you know that God used just three colors to make every color you see in the world? These colors are called primary colors. The word "primary" means "first," and the colors are called the primary colors because they are the first colors we need to make other colors. Can you say the word "primary" with me? Pause for children to respond. **Great! So God made all the other colors by mixing up the primary colors. We're going to see how that works.**

Hold up a clear plastic cup and a straw, and say: **I'm going to put some yellow water into this cup using a straw.** Show children how to put the straw into the yellow water, cover the top of the straw with a finger, and uncover the top of the straw over the empty cup. Demonstrate this several times so children understand how to do it.

Say: **Now let's make a different color. What do you think will happen if I add blue water to this yellow water?** Allow children to respond.

Say: **Let's see what happens! I'm going to add just one drop of blue**

• • • • • • • •

Teacher Tip

As a fun follow-up to this activity, have preschoolers mix three primary colors of modeling dough together to create different colors.

• • • • • • • •

14

water at a time and swish the cup a little to mix it. When you see a new color, put your hands on top of your head.

Drip blue water into the yellow water, and swish the cup. Hold up the cup so all the children can see the color transformation. When all the children's hands are on their heads, say: **Name that color!** After children have called out the color, say: **Isn't that neat? When we add blue to yellow, we make green! That's how God made all the different colors from the primary colors. You can mix your own colors, too.**

Gather children around the table. Point out the cups of colored water and the straws. Ask children to keep the straws with their own cups so they don't get mixed up. Explain that each child will mix colors in his or her own cups or ice-cube trays. Make sure children understand how to move the colored water into their own cups using the straws. Say: **Try to mix lots of different colors. You could mix up red and yellow in one cup, blue and yellow in another cup, and red and blue in another cup.**

As preschoolers work, help them remember different color combinations to try. Ask:
● **What different colors are you making?**
● **What colors do you like best? Why?**
● **Why do you think God made so many pretty colors for us?**

When children have finished, say: **Our God is amazing. From these primary colors, he made all the colors in the world! I'm glad God made so many pretty colors.**

Have children wash their hands; empty the water from all the cups.

2. Separating Colors

Set out the saucers or bowls, the paper towels, the water-based markers, and the pitcher of water.

Say: **We're going to try something else to show us how God made all the colors from the primary colors. Instead of putting colors together, we're going to take colors apart.**

Hand each child a paper towel, and show children how to fold their paper towels in half three times. Then show preschoolers how to use their markers to make two one-inch lines about one and a half inches from the base of their paper towels. The colored lines should be about one inch apart from each other so children can use two colors. Fill each child's saucer or bowl with about a quarter of an inch of water; then have children set their paper towels in their saucers.

Say: **It will take a little time for our colors to come apart, so let's play a fun game about the colors God made while we wait.**

3. I Spy

Have children sit in a circle. Say: **God made so many colors, and they are all around us. In fact, as I look around the room, I can see lots of colors. I'm going to tell you about something I see, so try to guess what it is.**

Choose an object in the room. Describe it to the children, beginning your description with "I spy something that is…" For example, you might choose a red ball and say, "I spy something that is small, round, and red."

Call on children to guess what you're describing. If necessary, add clues to the list. When a child correctly guesses what you're describing, point out the object for everyone to see. Then have all the children call out, for example, "Thank you, God, for making red!"

Have a child sitting next to you "spy" something for everyone to guess. Continue around the circle until every child has had a chance to spy.

Then say: **Colors are so fun to look at. I like looking around and seeing so many pretty colors. Now let's go back to the table and check our experiments.**

Lead children back to the table to look at their paper towels. If a child made a green line on a paper towel, he or she should now see smudges of blue, then green, then yellow. Ask:

● **What has happened to the colors on your paper towels?**
● **What different colors do you see now?**

Say: **The colors on your paper towels have separated, or come apart. When we put yellow and blue together, we make green. So when we take green apart, we see yellow and blue. God made all the colors from just a few colors, the primary colors. Our God is pretty amazing, isn't he?**

Now we'll look in the Bible to see some different colors God made.

Colors Are in the Bible

1. In the Beginning, God Made Colors

Set out the stacks of construction paper you compiled before class. If you have some books that contain colorful nature pictures, set them nearby.

Open the Bible to Genesis 1:1, and show children the page. Say: **A long time ago, God made the world. He took six days to do it. On the first day, God made part of the world; on the second day, God made another part of the world. By the sixth day, God had made the whole world.**

Hand each child a stack of construction paper. Say: **Now we're going to hear about what God made each day and think about the colors God saw.**

Read aloud Genesis 1:1-2a. Then say: **Oh, darkness! From your pile of colored paper, hold up the colors you think God saw when he looked at the world in the beginning when it was dark.** Let children respond. Then read aloud verses 3-5. Ask:

● **What kinds of colors do you think God saw after the first day?**

Have children hold up their papers. Then read aloud verses 6-8, and have children hold up the colors they think God saw on the second day. Then read aloud verses 9-13, and ask:

● **What are things God made on the third day?**
● **What colors do you think God saw on the third day?**

Continue in the same way for verses 14-19, 20-23, and 24-25.

If you brought in nature books, let children look at the different colors God used when he made the animals. Then read aloud verses 26-27, 31. Say: **God also made people with different colors.** Ask:

● **What different colors can we find on each other?**

Have children look around at hair, eyes, and even teeth and hold up the colors they see. Ask:

● **Why do you think God made people so many different colors?**
● **Why do you think God made so many different colors in the world?**
● **How do colors help us?**

Say: **God knew we would enjoy looking at colors, and he knew that colors would help us to see things better. The Bible tells us that on the seventh day, after God made the whole world, he rested. Maybe God was looking at all the beautifully colored things he had made.**

Next we'll hear about colorful surprises and enjoy colors that are fun to eat!

Set aside the construction paper squares for later use.

Teacher Tip

As children hold up colors of paper in this activity, praise them for their choices. Their vivid imaginations may cause them to choose colors you didn't think of, but there aren't right or wrong answers.

Teacher Tip

You may want to read only portions of the Scripture to preschoolers to keep the pace moving. For example, Genesis 1:11-12a says, "Then God said, 'Let the land produce plants and trees with seeds and fruit.' And it was so."

17

2. A Rainbow Snack

Set out the sliced fruit, graham crackers, cream cheese, plastic knives, and paper plates.

Say: **God made many colors for us to enjoy, and sometimes we see those colors in surprising places! For example, what colors do you usually see when you look at the sky at night?** Allow children to respond. **And what colors do you normally see when you look at the sky during the day?** Allow children to respond. **When we look at the sky at night, we usually see black with sparkling white stars and a yellow moon. When we look at the sky during the day, we usually see blue with white clouds. Every once in a while, though, God surprises us! Let's read in the Bible about a colorful surprise.**

Open the Bible to Genesis 9:8-16, and show preschoolers the passage. Say: **Once it rained so hard that the whole world was covered with water. After the world was dry again, God promised that he would never let it be covered with water again. To remind everyone of his promise, God made a colorful rainbow in the sky! How many of you have seen rainbows?** Allow children to respond. **It's so fun to see all those beautiful colors in the sky, isn't it? When we see colorful rainbows, we can remember that God loves us. To remind us of God's love, let's make a rainbow snack.**

Tell children that they each will get a paper plate, a graham cracker, some cream cheese, and a knife. Explain that children should first use the knife to spread the cream cheese on the cracker and then put some colorful fruit slices on top. When everyone understands, distribute the supplies. As children work, ask:

● **What do colorful rainbows help us remember about God?**
● **Why do you think God uses colorful rainbows to help us remember his promise?**

When children have finished making their snacks, say: **Rainbows can help us remember that God loves us. They can also help us remember that God made all the colors! The colors on these snacks make me want to eat them! First let's say together, "Thank you, God, for colors!"** Have children repeat the prayer with you and then eat their snacks.

When children have finished, have them wash their hands. As they do, clear off the table.

3. Color-Scopes

Set out the toilet paper tubes, cellophane squares, and rubber bands.
Say: **God made colors, so he must like colors too! In fact, God once**

told some people to put colors in a special church called a tabernacle. I'll read what God said to the people building the tabernacle while you listen for the colors God named. Read aloud Exodus 26:1a: "**Make the tabernacle with ten curtains of finely twisted linen and blue, purple and [red] yarn.**" Ask:

● **What colors did God want in his special church?**

● **Why do you think God wanted the special church to be colorful?**

Say: **Colors are fun! Even God likes colorful things. I wonder what the world would be like if everything were the same color. What if all the flowers and the grass and every dog and even our food were white? That wouldn't be very fun, would it? Let's see what it would be like if God had made everything one color.**

Show preschoolers how to wrap a piece of colored cellophane around the end of a toilet paper tube and then secure the cellophane with a rubber band.

Help children make their color-scopes. When everyone has finished, say: **Now look through your tube to see how the world looks when it's all one color.** Ask:

● **What does the world look like?**

● **Can you see everything as well when it's just one color?**

● **Would the world be as fun to look at if everything were just one color? Explain.**

Have children add another piece of cellophane to the first piece and look through. Then have children share color-scopes. Each time, ask children what the world looks like.

Say: **God loves us. He knew we would like colors, so he made lots and lots of different colors! I'm thankful that God made colors, aren't you? Let's thank God for making so many colors.**

Let's Thank God for Colors

1. Colorful Prayer

Set out the squares of construction paper you used earlier. Give each child one square of either green, yellow, brown, orange, red, or blue paper. Then have the children sit down.

Say: **We're going to say a prayer to God, thanking him for all the beautiful colors he made. As we say the prayer, you'll hear different colors. When we say the color of paper you're holding, stand up and hold your paper high.**

Thank you, God, for colors,
Like green and yellow and brown.
They're on the trees and flowers;
Your colors are all around.

Thank you, God, for colors,
Like orange, red, and blue.
We love all your colors,
And we love you, too.

Repeat the prayer, and have children sit when they hear their color. If you have time, say the prayer a few more times. After each prayer, allow children to trade papers with each other.

God Created Dirt and Rocks

Who praises God for mud? Not many people do. But Jesus said if we're silent, the stones will cry out (Luke 19:40)—and they do. All of God's creation is perfect in its design and purpose. Even the rocks and the dirt—the humble building blocks of our planet—shout the wonder of our creative God.

Many adults take little time to consider the marvelous stuff we trample over daily. But young children are fascinated with dirt. Children love to sift dirt, dig in the dirt, and track dirt onto our carpets. Young children often hear, "Don't get dirty." But in this lesson, preschoolers will touch and explore God's creation of dirt. They'll smell the pungent dirt, wiggle their fingers in silky sand, and sing a song about soil. Join the kids, and dig into this lesson. Together, you can unearth the treasures of God's handiwork.

Supply List

- a Bible
- newspaper
- large plastic bowls
- dirt or potting soil
- sand
- salt
- rocks
- a magnifying glass
- several small bowls of water
- talcum or baby powder
- one package of instant chocolate pudding mix for every four to six children
- a large plastic jar with a tight lid

- large resealable plastic bags
- milk
- measuring cups
- brownies
- vanilla wafers
- paper cups
- plastic spoons
- borax
- water
- cornstarch
- container with a tight lid
- plastic foam plates
- a permanent marker

Teacher Tip

Be sure all the rocks you bring to class are bigger than a half dollar. Smaller rocks are choking hazards for preschoolers.

Preparation

Cover a table with newspaper. Fill one unbreakable bowl with dirt or potting soil, another with sand, another with salt, and another with rocks. If you have a large class, fill enough bowls so that no more than three or four children share a bowl.

Make this pliable soil for the "Soil Sculpture" activity (p. 25). One recipe will supply four preschoolers. Mix 1/4 cup of borax with 3/4 cup of water. Also mix 1/4 cup of cornstarch into 1 cup of water. Microwave the cornstarch mixture until it thickens (start with one minute); then combine both mixtures. Add 2 cups of potting soil. Keep the mixture in a tightly covered container.

God Created Dirt and Rocks

1. Discover Dirt and Rocks!

Move chairs out from a table so children are able to easily walk around it; then spread newspaper on the table. At different spots around the table, set out the bowls of dirt or potting soil, sand, salt, and rocks.

Have children form a circle around the table. Then pick up a handful of dirt or potting soil, and say: **Oh, this dirt is soft and very crumbly between my fingers.** Put the handful of dirt back in the bowl, hold up your hands, and say: **And look! Now my hands are dirty. You can see the dirt on my hands.** Ask:

● **Why do you think God made dirt?**

● **What good things does dirt do?**

Say: **God put the dirt and rocks under our feet so we could have something good to walk on and something good to grow things in. On our table, we can see different kinds of dirt God made.**

Show children the bowl of potting soil. Say: **In dirt like this, plants and flowers and trees can grow. God gives us lots of dirt so we can have lots of plants!**

Show children the sand. **This kind of dirt is called sand. Has anyone ever played in a sandbox or with the sand near an ocean?** Pause for children to respond. **Crabs, clams, and other small animals live in the sand near the ocean. Sand is fun to play in, isn't it?**

Show children the bowl of salt, and ask: **Does this look like dirt?** Pause for children to respond, and then say: **This doesn't look like dirt because it's salt! Did you know that God put things like salt into the dirt? We use salt to make food taste better.**

Show children the rocks. **These rocks are just big pieces of dirt. Bugs and snakes live under rocks, and big rocks put together make mountains.** Ask:

● **Why do you think God made so many kinds of dirt?**

Say: **Each of these kinds of dirt has a different job to do, so God made all the kinds of dirt that we need.** Encourage the children to walk around the table and put their hands into the different kinds of dirt. Direct them to crumble the soil between their fingers and smell it, make lines and drawings in the sand, pour salt onto their palms and taste just a bit, and rub the rocks together and listen to the sounds they make. After several minutes of exploration, ask:

- **What kind of dirt is your favorite? Why?**
- **What good things does God do with dirt and rocks?**

Say: **God made all kinds of good dirt and rocks. Next we're going to have more fun with God's good dirt.**

2. Digging Deeper

Show children the magnifying glass. Say: **This is called a magnifying glass, and it helps us see very small things as though they were big! Let's see what the different kinds of dirt look like when you look through a magnifying glass.**

Have children take turns looking through the magnifying glass at the soil, sand, salt, and rocks. Then set out several small bowls of water near the rocks and the soil. Have children take turns plunking rocks into the water to see how they change color in the water. Also have children take turns adding a little water to a small pile of soil to make mud. Finally, have children each rub two rocks together to make powdery dirt.

Teacher Tip

You may want to recruit some help for this activity. Though not critical, additional adults can help guide children to discover more about dirt at each bowl.

Teacher Tip

If possible, provide several magnifying glasses. At thrift stores, you can often find inexpensive plastic reading magnifiers that work well for this activity.

Teacher Tip

Preschoolers love to do the unusual in the classroom. If you have time and don't mind a little extra cleanup, have children take off their shoes and socks and squiggle their toes around in the sand.

Say: **Dirt and rocks are special things. God made rocks, and he crushed up rocks to make sand. God made the dirt to do some very important jobs.**

Dirt holds seeds in the ground. Without the dirt, we wouldn't have any plants or food! We would be so hungry! Underneath all the grass and trees, God put great big rocks. The rocks hold us up. Even the smallest kind of rock that God made is very important. Open your hands, and I will give each of you a little of the softest kind of rock God made; it's called talcum. Can you say that with me? Pause as children respond. Pour a little talcum into each child's hands. Then say: **This is talcum. If you rub your hands together, it will take the sand off your hands. Talcum is so small and soft that it feels good on a baby's skin. Isn't God amazing? The rocks God made can be hard like these rocks, squishy like this dirt, tiny like this sand, tasty like this salt, and soft like this powder. I'm glad God is so creative, aren't you?**

3. Dirt Dessert

Have children wash their hands. Then say: **Let's make a dirt dessert! Of course, you never want to eat real dirt or put rocks into your mouth, but we'll make a yummy snack that looks like dirt and pretend it's mud, sand, and rocks.**

Pour the dry pudding mix into the plastic jar, and add two cups of cold milk. Close the jar securely, and let the children help you shake the jar. Ask:

● **What did we add to the dry powder to make it wet?**
● **What does God add to dirt to make it mud?**

Set the jar of pudding aside for about five minutes. Give each child half a brownie to squish into balls as rocks. Put a few vanilla wafers in a resealable plastic bag, and securely seal the bag. Say: **To make sand, God crushed some rocks up. Let's pretend these cookies are rocks and crush them until they're sand.** Give each child a turn to crush the cookies.

Scoop the pudding into paper cups. Let preschoolers sprinkle some "sand" on top and then plop a few brownie rocks in. Give each child a spoon. While the children are eating, ask:

● **What good things do dirt and rocks do?**

Say: **God made the dirt and the rocks to do good things. We build things like houses with rocks. God made big mountains with rocks. Plants grow in the dirt. I'm glad God made the rocks and the dirt.**

Dirt and Rocks Are in the Bible

1. Soil Sculptures

Say: **God says dirt is really special. God talks about dirt in his book, the Bible. Listen closely to this verse about dust. Dust is another word for dirt.** Read aloud Genesis 2:7: **"The Lord God formed the man from the dust of the ground and breathed into his nostrils the breath of life, and man became a living being."** Ask:

● **Who made man?**

● **Why do you think God made the first man out of dirt?**

Say: **We can make things out of soft, squishy dirt. But God made the very first man in the world out of dirt! That's amazing, isn't it? Let's make things out of the dirt now.**

Write each child's name on a plastic foam plate with a permanent marker. Give each child a handful of the pliable soil mixture, and encourage kids to make something out of the dirt.

When children have finished, have them set aside their creations to dry, and then wash their hands. Then say: **God could have made the first man out of anything, but he made the first man out of dirt. That tells us that God can do anything!**

2. The House on the Rock

Say: **The Bible also tells us that the rocks God made keep us safe.** Open a Bible to Matthew 7:24-25, and show the passage to the children while you say: **Jesus told a story about a man who built a house on rocks because he knew the rocks would keep him and his house safe. While I tell you the story, you're going to make sounds that go with the story. The man in our story will build a house. When you build a house, you do lots of hammering. You can all make hammering sounds by stomping your feet on the floor. Let's try it.** Have the children stomp on the floor.

Say: **Those are great hammering sounds! Now listen while I tell the story, and we'll make some different sounds.**

A man we'll call Work-Hard-Rocky needed to build a house, but he wasn't sure where to build it. Rocky loved to swim and wanted to build his house near the water. Do you think Rocky should build his house in the water? Pause for children to respond. **No, Rocky didn't want to be wet all the time! Should Rocky build his house on top of a tree beside the water?** Pause for children to respond. **It would be fun to have a tree house, but Rocky wanted his house to be on the safest spot possible. "Aha!" thought Rocky. "God made rocks very strong. My house will be safe on a big, strong rock." So Rocky found a big, strong rock near the water and started building his house.**

Work-Hard-Rocky hammered and hammered and hammered. Have the children make hammering sounds. **It was hard work, building a house on top of that rock. Rocky worked for a long time.** Have the children make hammering sounds again. **Just as Rocky finished building his house, he heard some thunder. Let's pound our fists on the floor to make thunder.** Allow children to respond. **"It's going to rain," Rocky said. "I sure am glad I built my house on this rock. God made rocks big and strong, so I know I'll be safe." Soon Rocky heard the pitter, patter, pitter, patter of raindrops. Let's make raindrops by drumming our fingers on the floor.** Allow children to respond. **Rocky went inside his house that he had built on rock and waited. It rained and thundered for a long time, but Rocky wasn't scared. He knew that God made the rocks big and strong. He knew he was safe because he had built his house on the big, strong rock. And do you know what? That big storm passed by, and Rocky *was* safe in his house on the rock!**

Congratulate the kids for their sound effects. Ask:

● **Why was Rocky's house safe?**
● **What other things can God's rocks do?**

Say: **God made the dirt and rocks. He gives us everything we need. God's rocks are big and strong and can keep us safe.**

3. The Good Soil

Say: **Another story in the Bible tells us about good dirt.** Open the Bible to Luke 8:5-8a, and hold up the passage for preschoolers to see. Say: **In this story, Jesus tells about a man who tried to plant some seeds to grow some plants. What does the man need to make his seeds grow into plants?** Allow children to respond. **He needs sunshine and water, and he also needs the good dirt God made. But when the man planted his seeds, some fell into the road. Do you think the plants grew in the road?** Allow children to respond. **No, some birds ate the seeds in the road. Next the man planted some seeds on rocks. Do you think the plants grew in the rocks?** Allow children to respond. **No, the rocks were too hard for the seeds, and the plants didn't grow. Some other seeds fell on some sticker bushes. Do you think the plants grew in the sticker bushes?** Allow children to respond. **No, they couldn't grow well in the sticker bushes. But some seeds fell in the good soil, which is another name for dirt. Let's hear what the Bible says about that.** Read aloud Luke 8:8: **"Still other seed fell on good soil. It came up and yielded a crop, a hundred times more than was sown." That means the seeds that fell in the good soil grew lots and lots of plants.** Ask:

● **How does dirt help plants?**

Say: **The dirt helps plants to grow. I sure am glad God made the dirt! Let's thank God now for making the dirt and rocks.**

Let's Thank God for Dirt and Rocks

1. Thank You for Dirt and Rocks

Retrieve one of the rocks that the children used in the first part of the lesson. Have preschoolers stand in a circle. Explain that you're going to say a poem that's also a prayer to thank God for making dirt and rocks. Say: **Every time you hear the word "dirt" or the word "rock," pass this rock to the next person in the circle.**

Hand the rock to the first child, and say this poem prayer; the rhyme is patterned after "Head, Shoulders, Knees, and Toes."

> **We thank you, God, for dirt and rocks, dirt and rocks.**
> **We thank you, God, for dirt and rocks, dirt and rocks.**
> **Dirt and rocks are God's building blocks.**
> **We thank you, God, for dirt and rocks, dirt and rocks.**

Repeat the rhyme a few times, and encourage children to join in. Then retrieve the rock, and close with a prayer like this one: **Dear God, thank you for loving us so much that you think of everything we need—even dirt and rocks. Amen.**

God Created Heat

What does heat feel like? Like a hot bath, a warm blanket, a fuzzy pet, or a cup of steamy hot chocolate! God created heat from energy to help things work and grow. The many chemical reactions taking place inside us create heat that keeps us warm. In short, heat keeps us warm and helps us function.

Young children love to snuggle under blankets; cuddle a soft, warm pet; and nestle into a cozy hug. As preschoolers explore heat in this lesson, they'll learn through playful activities that God made heat because he loves us and wants the world to be a good place for us to live in.

Supply List

- a Bible
- newspaper
- two dishpan-sized plastic tubs
- a few water toys or unbreakable kitchen utensils, such as measuring cups and spoons
- warm water and cold water
- old crayons
- crayon sharpener, pencil sharpener, or grater
- a muffin tin or sandwich bags
- construction paper or tissue paper
- scissors
- yarn
- wax paper
- an iron
- a heating pad

- one small, healthy houseplant and one small, withered or yellowed houseplant
- an electric blanket or other warm blanket
- quart-size resealable plastic bags
- instant hot chocolate mix
- miniature marshmallows
- powdered nondairy creamer
- measuring spoons
- tape
- plastic foam cups
- a label from the "Just for You" handout (p. 36) for each child
- a hole punch
- newsprint

Teacher Tip

If you don't have a withered or yellowed houseplant, put a houseplant in a dark room a few days before class. You can water the plant, but don't give it any sunlight. It should look withered or yellowed in time for the class.

29

Preparation

Use old crayons and a crayon sharpener, pencil sharpener, or hand grater to make crayon shavings. Each child will need one or two tablespoons of shavings. Keep colors separate in a muffin tin or sandwich bags. Also cut one sixteen-inch piece of yarn for each child. Cut a one-inch heart out of construction paper or tissue paper for each child.

On the "Just for You" handout (p. 36), fill in the amount of water needed according to the instructions for the hot chocolate mix you use. Make photocopies of the drink mix instructions on colored paper, and cut out the labels. Punch a hole in the upper left-hand corner of each label. You'll need one label per child.

God Created Heat

1. Exploring Heat

Teacher Tip

You may want to provide several tubs depending on how many children you're expecting.

Set a tub of warm water and a few water toys on a table covered with newspaper. Allow children to play in the water as they enter the room.

As children are playing in the water, say: **Isn't this water warm? I love warm water! Today we're going to learn that God made heat because he loves us and wants us to be healthy and warm.** Ask:

● **What would it be like if we didn't have hot water and had to take cold baths?**

● **What are some other things that are hot besides this water?**

Say: **God gave us many hot things. I love cookies out of the oven, warm coats, and lots of hugs! Let's see how warm water is different from cold water.**

Set out a tub of cold water. Have children touch the outsides of the tubs. Ask:

● **How do the tubs feel different?**

Allow the children to play in both tubs of water. Encourage children to go from the warm water to the cold water and then back to the warm water. Ask:

● **How do your hands feel when you go from the warm water to the cold water? from the cold water to the warm water?**

● **Tell me about a time you were cold and what you did to warm up.**

Say: **Have you ever been very, very cold and your mom or dad had you take a hot bath? At first the water feels hot! Then pretty soon it**

feels just right. And if you stay in the water longer, it starts to feel cold! That's because your body warms up. God gives us warm things to keep us from getting too cold. Heat keeps us safe and healthy.

2. Melting Hearts

In the middle of the table covered with newspaper, set the crayon shavings and the paper hearts. Give each child a piece of yarn and two 12x12-inch pieces of wax paper. Place the iron out of the children's reach, and turn it to a low setting.

Say: **Now we're going to use heat to be artists! Watch while I show you what to do.** Sprinkle some crayon shavings in the center of a piece of wax paper. Then loop a piece of yarn in half, and lay it in the middle of the paper with the looped end hanging off the edge of the paper. Add a paper heart and a few more crayon shavings. Cover all of this with another piece of wax paper.

Show children the iron, and ask:

● **What do you think will happen when I put this hot iron on the wax paper?**

Teacher Tip

Be sure to let each child watch while you're heating his or her picture. This will help preschoolers make the connection between the heat God gave us and making something pretty with the heat.

Say: **Let's try it and see.** Lay a piece of newsprint over the wax paper, and press with the warm iron. Set the iron aside, away from children's reach. Remove the newsprint, and hold up the wax paper. Ask:

● **What happened to the crayon shavings? Why?**
● **What other things can heat melt?**

Say: **When my paper is cool, I'm going to cut around the melted design and hang it up in the window. It will remind me that God loves us so much that he made heat! Now it's your turn to be an artist.**

Help children assemble their own materials. As children work, say: **God made the heat because he loves you and me. You are all doing a wonderful job using heat to make something pretty.** Have an adult helper assist the children while you begin ironing the children's projects one by one. Set aside each picture to cool.

When the papers are cool, cut around the melted crayon designs. Give children the option of hanging them in a classroom window or taking them home.

Teacher Tip

If an outlet isn't
located near your
story area, use a
hot water bottle or
an extension cord.
Be sure to put
away the heating
pad and extension
cord when you've
finished so
preschoolers don't
trip.

3. We Can Make Things Warm

Turn the heating pad on medium, and set it near you.

Have children sit around you on the floor. Say: **God is so good. He made heat because he loves us. When our hands are cold, how can we warm them up?** Allow children to respond. **There are many ways we can warm our hands, aren't there? We can hold them against our cheeks, put them in warm water, or put on mittens. Right now, let's all hold hands to warm them up.**

Have children form a circle and hold hands. Say: **While we're holding hands, we can sing a song telling God, "Thank you for making heat."**

Sing the following song to the tune of "God Is So Good."

> **God made the heat.**
> **God made the heat.**
> **God made the heat**
> **To keep us safe and warm.**

Then say: **Let's sit down now and do something else to warm up our hands.** Set the heating pad where everyone can reach it, and say: **Ahh, a hot heating pad can warm us up!** Sing "God Made the Heat" again while the children warm their hands. Then unplug the heating pad, and set it aside. Ask:

● **What's your favorite way to warm up when you're cold?**

Then say: **God loves us and keeps us safe and healthy with heat. Let's learn about some other ways we use heat.**

Heat Is in the Bible

1. God Made the Sun

Set the houseplants nearby.

Open the Bible to Psalm 19, and say: **The Bible tells us about something God made that gives us heat. Listen and see if you know what it is.**

Read Psalm 19:1, 4b, 6 (NCV): **"The heavens tell the glory of God, and the skies announce what his hands have made...The sky is like a home for the sun...The sun rises at one end of the sky and follows its path to the other end. Nothing hides from its heat."** Ask:

● **What did God make that gives us heat?**

Say: **God made the sun to give us heat! The sun keeps us warm and helps us to grow. Here's something else that grows because of the sun.**

Hold up the healthy plant, and say: **The sun helps this plant to grow. But look what happens to plants if they don't get any sun.** Hold up the withered plant, and say: **This poor plant didn't get enough light! Almost everything that lives needs the sun for light and warmth. God made the sun because he loves us and wants us to grow.**

Set the plants aside, and say: **Let's stand up and play a game. I'm going to call out some words. If the word I say is something that needs the sun to grow, stand up tall on your tiptoes, and reach for the sky as though you're trying to touch the sun. If the word I say is something that doesn't need the sun, wilt like our withered plant and droop down low to the floor. If I say "chair," what would you do? You would droop because a chair isn't a growing thing. It doesn't need the sun.**

Name things such as tree, dog, house, baby, flower, ball, book, garden, car, cat, and bird. When you've finished playing the game, say: **You all did so well! I'm glad God made the sun to give us heat!**

2. All Heated Up

Plug in the electric blanket, and turn it on so it gets warm.

Open the Bible to Ecclesiastes 4:11, and say: **Did you know that the Bible talks about snuggling? It's true! Listen to what it says in the book of Ecclesiastes. "If two lie down together, they will keep warm. But how can one keep warm alone?" Let's all snuggle together in one big hug.**

Gather the children together in a group hug, and say: **If we stayed like this, we'd keep each other warm!** Hold up the electric blanket, and say: **Here's another way some people keep warm.**

Let children feel the electric blanket. Say: **Let's play a game with our warm blanket. Someone will be "It." "It" will warm up underneath the electric blanket. When I ask "It," "Are you toasty?" "It" will say, "I'm toasty!" and will run to someone and hug him or her. Then both of them will warm up under the blanket. When I ask again, "Are you toasty?" they'll answer, "We're toasty!" Then they'll each run and hug someone and bring both of them back to the blanket.**

Play the game until everyone is part of the blanket hug. Turn off the blanket, and ask:

● **How did you feel when you got all those hugs?**

● **How did the blanket make you feel?**

Say: **Hugs can make us feel warm inside and outside. I don't know about you, but I'm warm!**

Teacher Tip

If you didn't have time to let a plant wither in the dark, use a dried-out or dying plant from your yard, or simply talk with the children about what would happen if the plant didn't get any light.

Teacher Tip

If it's hot, use a regular blanket instead of an electric blanket. Point out that even if it's hot when we go to bed, the air usually cools off in the middle of the night because the sun is gone. Then we need our blankets to make us warm 'til the sun heats things up again.

Teacher Tip

Be sure the hot water isn't hot enough to burn the children. Most preschoolers will probably prefer lukewarm hot chocolate, which will still teach them about heat.

Teacher Tip

To save time in this activity, make the hot chocolate for the children ahead of time, and bring it to class in a large thermos. Children can add the marshmallows.

Teacher Tip

If it's too hot, sit on top of the blanket and don't plug it in. Point out that God made ways for us to be warm or cool, whichever we need.

3. Be Warmed and Be Filled

Set out the resealable bags, instant hot chocolate mix, miniature marshmallows, powdered creamer, and measuring spoons.

Say: **When we eat warm food, it warms us up. Food gives us energy and helps us grow. Listen to what the Bible says about warmth and food in the book of James.** Read aloud James 2:15-16, and then say: **This verse tells us that Jesus wants us to help others keep warm. We're going to make gift bags of hot chocolate mix to give away. Then we'll make some for ourselves, too.**

Give each child a resealable bag. Help preschoolers put enough hot chocolate mix for one serving in each bag, according to package instructions. Help children add one tablespoon of powdered creamer and a few marshmallows to their bags. Seal the bags, and tape a label from the "Just for You" handout (p. 36) to each bag. Then set aside the bags.

Distribute plastic foam cups, and help children make some mix for themselves. When everyone is ready, have an adult add warm water to the cups. When the hot chocolate is cool enough, let children drink. Encourage children to hold the cups in their hands and feel the heat. Say: **Our cups of hot chocolate are warming our hands. When we drink it, our tummies will warm up too. As you drink your hot chocolate, let's talk about who we'll give our gift bags to.** Have children talk about people they love who might need or want hot chocolate. Praise children for making someone else warm and happy. Say: **I'm so glad God gives us heat. And with our hot chocolate gift bags, we can give heat to others!**

Let's Thank God for Heat

1. Warm Prayers

Have children sit in a circle. Spread the electric blanket over the laps of everyone in the circle. Plug in the electric blanket, turn it on, and say: **God made heat for us. Today we've learned many ways we use heat. I just plugged this blanket in, and it's warming up.** Ask:

● **Why do you think God made heat?**
● **How do we use the heat God gave us?**

Say: **God gave us heat because he loves us. We use heat to keep warm, to make things grow, to cook our food, and even to make pretty things. Let's thank God for making heat. Hold the hands of the friends sitting next to you and keep them under our warm blanket. I'll start by thanking God for something hot. Then I'll squeeze the person's hand on my right. That means I'm finished praying and it's his** (or her) **turn** to pray. **When you finish praying, squeeze the next person's hand.**

Help children thank God for such things as the sun, warm baths, food, and pets. If a child is shy about praying, have him or her—or the whole group—simply say, "Thank you, God, for heat."

When everyone has had a chance to pray, say: **Those were good prayers. God made heat for us, and it is good. Before we go, let's sing our song one more time.** Sing "God Made the Heat" to the tune of "God Is So Good."

God made the heat.
God made the heat.
God made the heat
To keep us safe and warm.

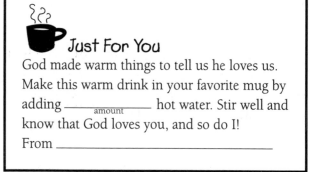 **Just For You**

God made warm things to tell us he loves us.
Make this warm drink in your favorite mug by
adding _____ hot water. Stir well and
               amount
know that God loves you, and so do I!
From _____

Just For You

God made warm things to tell us he loves us.
Make this warm drink in your favorite mug by
adding _____ hot water. Stir well and
               amount
know that God loves you, and so do I!
From _____

 Just For You

God made warm things to tell us he loves us.
Make this warm drink in your favorite mug by
adding _____ hot water. Stir well and
               amount
know that God loves you, and so do I!
From _____

 Just For You

God made warm things to tell us he loves us.
Make this warm drink in your favorite mug by
adding _____ hot water. Stir well and
               amount
know that God loves you, and so do I!
From _____

 Just For You

God made warm things to tell us he loves us.
Make this warm drink in your favorite mug by
adding _____ hot water. Stir well and
               amount
know that God loves you, and so do I!
From _____

 Just For You

God made warm things to tell us he loves us.
Make this warm drink in your favorite mug by
adding _____ hot water. Stir well and
               amount
know that God loves you, and so do I!
From _____

Just For You

God made warm things to tell us he loves us.
Make this warm drink in your favorite mug by
adding _____ hot water. Stir well and
               amount
know that God loves you, and so do I!
From _____

Just For You

God made warm things to tell us he loves us.
Make this warm drink in your favorite mug by
adding _____ hot water. Stir well and
               amount
know that God loves you, and so do I!
From _____

God Created the Land

Psalm 96 says all the earth glorifies the Lord; everything God made testifies that he is creative and powerful. The Bible even says that different land forms praise God—mountains and forests and valleys sing; the desert and hills are glad. Just as the land praises God, we can praise God for the land's beauty and bounty.

Preschoolers love to learn about new places. Seeing the mountains for the first time, one little girl said, "What country is *this?*" She just couldn't believe that the rocks rising toward the sky could exist in the same country as the rolling hills and grasslands she normally saw. The fascination children hold for land even extends into play: Children love to pretend they're in a forest, on a sandy island, or high on a mountain-top. In this lesson, children will discover that God created all kinds of land and will praise him along with the forests and hills.

Supply List

- a Bible
- blocks
- scissors
- sandpaper
- fabric scraps
- cotton balls
- Easter grass
- a bowl of puffed rice cereal
- cups of glue
- Q-Tips cotton swabs
- construction paper
- chalk
- napkins
- bread
- shakers of cinnamon sugar
- spoons
- jelly

Preparation

Warm the jelly to room temperature.

God Created Land

1. An Imaginary Journey

After the children have arrived, have them gather around you. Say:
Today we're going to talk about the land, which means mountains

and hills and valleys. Let's think of as many different kinds of land as we can. Help the children think of land forms, such as plains, forests, deserts, beaches, and swamps. Ask:

- **What kind of land do we live on?**
- **What other kinds of land have you seen?**

Say: **Let's go on an imaginary journey to see the land God made.**

Tell children that they should follow you and mimic what you do. Begin your exploration by saying: **First we're going to walk across the plains. The plains are very flat, so the walk should be easy!** Walk forward with long, peppy strides. **I can see for miles and miles.** Shield your eyes with your hands, and pretend to look into the distance all around you. **Because there are no hills or mountains to block the wind, it's getting really windy here on the plains. Maybe this walk isn't going to be as easy as I thought!** Lean forward and slow your walk, pretending to walk against a strong wind. **Whew! Walking against the wind is making me tired. It looks as though we're almost through the plains, but we have to walk across a desert next.**

OK, we're in the desert now. The desert is so dry and hot. There are no trees for shade, and it's still pretty windy. Shade your eyes with your hands and walk, leaning forward as though walking into the wind. **Whew! It's so hot and dry in the desert that very few plants or animals live here.** Fan your face with your hand. **And the ground isn't grassy; it's sandy. My feet keep sliding in the sand.** Shuffle your feet as if walking is difficult. **I'm getting thirsty, so I hope we get to the end of the desert soon.** Rub your throat. **Does anyone see water?** Allow children to answer. **I see water! Let's run to it and get a drink.** Jog a few steps, and then bend down and pretend to drink handfuls of water. Stand up and walk a few steps.

Now we're entering a forest, and we'll find some shade here. Forests are filled with trees! Point and look up. **There are so many trees that it's actually a little dark in here.** Hold your hands in front as if feeling your way through. **I hear lots of animal sounds. What kinds of animals do you hear as we walk through the forest?** Allow children to respond. **In the forest, there are also lots of plants, bushes, small trees, and tree trunks lying around on the ground. We'd better be careful not to trip over anything or walk into anything.** Step high as if stepping over things, and duck as if walking under things. **It's getting lighter, so we must be at the end of the forest. We're going to climb a mountain next!**

Here we are at the bottom of the mountain. Look how high we'll climb. Point and look up. **This mountain is pretty rocky, so we'll have to climb carefully.** Step high, and use your arms as if climbing a steep mountain.

Look how far we've come; it's a long way down. Look down over your shoulder. **We're so high that the air is cooler here. I'm getting a little cold.** Shiver and rub your arms. **We're at the top! I'm glad because I'm tired and cold.** Sit down, and have the children gather around you. Ask:

- **What kinds of things did you see as we explored?**
- **What was your favorite part of our walk? Why?**

Say: **God made all the land. God is smart enough to make tall mountains, cool forests, and hot deserts. God is wonderful!**

2. My Favorite Land

Say: **Let's learn a song about all the types of land God made.** Ask:

- **Of all the different kinds of land we named, which is your favorite? Why?**

Have children make up motions to describe their favorite land forms. For mountains, a child could form a "peak" with his or her arms. For swamps, a child could pretend his or her arms were the mouth of a crocodile.

Have the children stand in a circle. Explain that they'll sing the song together and take turns calling out a type of land and performing the motions they made.

Help the children learn the words to the following song, and then sing it together to the tune of "Pop! Goes the Weasel!"

> **From north to south, from east to west,**
> **God made the land.**
> **This is the land that I like best:**
> [Land form] **are my favorite!**

Sing the song together, and give each child a chance to call out a type of land and perform a motion. Go around the circle several times if the children want to show off different motions. Then have the children sit down. Ask:

- **Why do you think God made so many different kinds of land?**

Say: **God made so many different kinds of land, and they're all special. The amazing thing is that he's still changing the land every day! Let's find out how.**

3. God Is Still Creating

Say: **We're going to play a building game to find out two ways God changes the land. First you need to know what two words mean.** Ask:

- **Can anyone tell us what an earthquake is?**

● **Can anyone tell us what erosion is?**

Say: **In an earthquake, the land beneath us moves.** Hold up two blocks, and hold them against each other. Say: **The land in some places is like these blocks. When one block moves** (move one block away), **the land changes.**

The land also changes because of erosion. Place three blocks on top of each other, and hold them up. Say: **Erosion means that wind and water are wearing away parts of the land.** Take away one block. **Little by little, the land changes.** Take away another block. **Earthquakes make the land change suddenly, but erosion is very, very slow. We'll use earthquakes and erosion in a relay.**

Have the children form teams of about six members. Have the teams line up single file at one end of the room; then place an equal number of blocks for each team at the other end of the room. Provide *at least* one block for each team member. Explain that each team will build a mountain with its blocks and then erode the mountain. The first child on each team will run to the blocks, set up one block, and run back. The second child will run to the blocks, set a second block on top of the first, and run back. Teams will continue until all the blocks are stacked. When all of a team's blocks are stacked, the team will yell "Erosion!" Then they'll continue running the relay by taking blocks off the stack until the mountain is gone. If the blocks fall down any time during the process, the team will yell "Earthquake!" and will start either building again or eroding again.

When the children understand how to play, begin the game. After all the mountains have been eroded, have the children sit down. Ask:

● **How do earthquakes and erosion change the land?**

Say: **God made the land a long, long time ago, but God is still changing the land with things like earthquakes and erosion.**

Land Is in the Bible

1. Land Pictures

Say: **Now let's learn what the Bible says about the land God made.**

Open a Bible to Psalm 65:12-13, and show the passage to the children. Say: **As I read aloud from the Bible, listen carefully so you can tell me five different kinds of land it talks about.** Read aloud the Scripture. Ask the children to name the different kinds of land (grasslands, deserts, hills, meadows, valleys). Then say: **These verses tell us that the land praises God!**

● **How do you think the land shouts for joy and sings?**

Say: **God made the land, and land shows us how creative and**

wonderful God is. It's as if the land praises God! Let's celebrate by making pictures of all the kinds of land we just read about.

On a table, set out the scissors, sandpaper, fabric scraps, cotton balls, Easter grass, cereal, glue, and Q-Tips. Ask:

● **What could you use to make grasslands? deserts? hills clothed with gladness? meadows covered with sheep? valleys full of grain?**

Hand each child a piece of construction paper. Then help children use the Q-Tips to glue different items on their papers. When a child has finished his or her picture, use chalk to write the child's name and the words "God Made the Land" on the construction paper.

Teacher Tip

You may want an adult helper to assist with this activity. Most preschoolers will need help with cutting and gluing.

After everyone has finished, say: **What beautiful pictures you made!** Ask:

● **How do your pictures show that God made the land? that the land praises God?**

Say: **Your pictures can remind you that God made the land and that the land reminds us how good God is.** Have the children set aside their pictures.

2. Mountains Sing for Joy

Say: **Another verse in the Bible tells us that the land praises God.**

Hold up a Bible, and read aloud Psalm 98:8b: **"Let the mountains sing together for joy."** Ask:

● **What song do you think a mountain would sing to God?**

● **How do you like to praise God?**

Say: **Let's praise God as the mountains do. The Bible says the mountains sing together for joy.** Ask:

● **What kinds of noises do you think you would hear on a mountain?**

Help children think of noises such as whistling wind, rushing waterfalls, falling rocks, chattering squirrels, and creaking trees. Then say: **Now let's pretend that we all form a mountain. Then we'll make the noises of a mountain to sing praises to God.**

Have the children stand in two lines to form a V shape to look like a mountain. Then help each child decide a noise to make and a motion to do. For example, a child could be the wind blowing through the trees by bending from side to side, waving his or her arms, and making a "shh" noise.

After each child has chosen a noise and a motion, say: **Now let's sing our joyful praises to God as a mountain does.** Encourage all the children to make their noises and do their motions together. After several seconds, quiet the children, and ask:

● **Do you think this is how the mountains sing their praises to God?**

● **How do people sing their praises to God?**

Say: **Even if the mountains don't sing with voices as people do, mountains remind us of how wonderful and powerful God is.**

3. Desert Dessert

Have the children wash their hands and then gather around a table. Read aloud Isaiah 35:1, and then say: **It's very hot and dry in the desert. Sometimes, though, it rains in the desert. When it does, plants and flowers grow, and it's very pretty. Our Bible verse tells us that God made all the land beautiful. Let's make a yummy snack to remind us of the beautiful flowers that grow in the desert after the rain.**

Set out napkins, bread, shakers of cinnamon sugar, spoons, and warm jelly. Stir the jelly so it won't come out of the jar in big blobs.

Explain that the bread will be the land and the cinnamon sugar will be the sand that covers the desert. Show the children how to put a slice of bread on a napkin and gently shake cinnamon sugar onto the bread. Then explain that the jelly will be the flowers that bloom in the desert after it rains. Show the children how to use the spoon to place a couple of jelly dollops onto the bread.

Have the children work in groups of three. One child can place three slices of bread onto three napkins. The second child can sprinkle the cinnamon sugar onto the slices of bread. Then the third child can place dollops of jelly onto the slices of bread.

After the groups have finished making their treats, let kids sit down to eat. Don't forget to have the children wash their hands after they gobble up their snacks!

Let's Thank God for Land

1. God Is Grand!

Have children form a circle. Say: **One way we can praise God and thank him for making the land is to pray. Let's thank God for creating all the kinds of land we can think of.**

Teach the children to say, "God is great. God is grand. Let us thank him for our land." Tell children that they'll repeat those lines and then take turns naming different kinds of land they're thankful for.

Ask the children to join hands for the prayer. Say the rhyme together, and begin by naming a more unusual kind of land, such as deserts or swamps. Then allow the children to take turns naming types of land.

God Created Life

Has a grubby little hand ever handed you a weed bouquet? Have you ever heard an excited, "I caught one!" and suddenly found yourself holding a slightly squished grasshopper? Children are fascinated by all forms of life. But they need to know that God created living things and greatly values them.

In this lesson, preschoolers will use their imaginations, their observation and thinking skills, and their artistic expression to explore and respond to God's world of living things. They will grunt like pigs and flutter like butterflies. They will taste fruit and learn how a sea otter sleeps. They will use their breath to make water bubbles and to praise the giver of life, God. Every step of the way, children will appreciate God's loving care for living things.

Supply List

- a Bible
- two pipe cleaners
- a thin belt, preferably with a rough texture
- a large cotton ball
- a photocopy of the "Plant Life" handout (p. 51) for each child
- starfish pattern (p.45)
- crayons
- scissors
- construction paper
- paper plates
- clear adhesive paper
- silver, blue, or clear glitter
- hole punch
- yarn
- doll
- cups
- a pitcher of water
- straws
- fruit such as apple slices, banana slices, orange sections, or pineapple tidbits

Preparation

Fold two pipe cleaners in half, and twist them together to make a caterpillar. Then read the first activity so you're familiar with the script, and place the pipe cleaner "caterpillar," belt "snake," and cotton ball "rabbit" in a pocket or other safe, convenient place.

Using construction paper and the pattern, make one "starfish" for each child. Then for each child, cut the center out of a paper plate, and cut two circles of clear adhesive paper approximately one-half inch larger in diameter than the hole in the plate.

God Created Life

1. Animal Adventure Safari

Gather the children around you, and say: **Today we're going on a very special adventure. How many of you like to go on adventures?** Pause. **You're going to need some special glasses for our adventure. They're called make-believe glasses, and everyone already has a pair!** Show children how to hold their hands in circles around their eyes. Say: **Can you show me your make-believe glasses? They'll help you see some of the life God has made. Now let's line up and hold onto each other's waists!**

Take your place at the head of the "train." Shuffle your feet to slowly move forward without breaking the train. After a few steps, say: **We're at our first stop. We didn't have to go far—just into our backyard. Some wonderful living things that God made live very close to us. I think I see one now flying into the bushes. It's a bird called a cardinal. Can you see him with your make-believe glasses? He's bright red. Listen, he's talking to us. He says, "Sweet-sweet-sweet-sweet-sweet." Let's talk back to him in cardinal talk.** Encourage the children to say, "Sweet-sweet-sweet-sweet-sweet" with you.

Say: **I know where to find another of God's neat living things. It's**

right under this leaf. Pretend to turn over a leaf, and bring out the pipe cleaner caterpillar. **Here she is. This funny bug is called a caterpillar. If we're very gentle, we can pet her.** Pass around the pipe cleaner caterpillar for children to pet. **Did you know that if we come back in a few weeks, the caterpillar won't look the same? Does anybody know why?** Allow children to respond. **As this caterpillar grows, she'll change into a butterfly. Oh, look! There's one now.** Point in front of you. **Do you still have your make-believe glasses on? Look how the butterfly flaps her wings. Let's pretend to be butterflies.** Allow children to pretend to be butterflies.

OK. **Everybody back in line. It's time to leave our backyard and find more of God's wonderful living things.** Lead children for a few steps again, and then say: **Now we're in the woods. The animals that live here are very shy. We'll have to look carefully. I see something.** Point toward the ground. **It's a garter snake.** Pass around the belt "snake." **Can you feel how rough his skin is? It protects him as he slides on the ground. Oh, look at his tongue. He's flicking it in and out. Let's flick our tongues back at him.** Lead children in flicking their tongues.

I see another animal. It's a rabbit. I think she's going to let us pet her. Pass around the cotton ball "rabbit." **Let's see if we can hop like she does. Hold your hands in front of you like paws, and put your feet together. Now jump forward a few times.** Lead the children in hopping a few times. **You did it! It's time to move on. Let's get back into our line.**

Lead children for a few steps, and then say: **Here we are at the farm! I see a pig; he's cooling off by rolling in the mud.** Can you see him with your make-believe glasses? **Listen! He's talking to us. Let's talk back in pig talk.** Encourage children to grunt or oink with you. **Everyone wave goodbye, and then get back into our line.**

As you lead children, say: **For our last stop, let's go to Africa. Look! There's a lion!** Point in the distance. **We can't get too close, but I think we can hear him. He's roaring at us. Let's roar back.** Encourage children to roar like a lion.

Say: **Well, it's time for us to take off our glasses and end our adventure. Here we are back in our classroom.** Ask:

● **What was your favorite thing we saw?**

Allow time for children to answer; then say: **God made everything we saw with our make-believe glasses. Not only did God make them, but he also gave them life. When I think about all those different animals God made and gave life to, I want to tell God that he did a great job. If you think God did a great job, clap with me, and say, "Great job, God!"** Lead children in clapping and cheering for God.

Teacher Tip

For extra fun, bring in a stuffed rabbit for children to pet.

2. Plant Sequence Pictures

Have children sit at tables; set out the scissors, crayons, and "Plant Life" handouts (p. 51). Say: **God also made plants. Plants are alive even though they don't move or make noises like animals. We know plants are alive because they grow. Look at the first picture on your paper. It's a seed. A seed doesn't look like it's alive, but God gives seeds life. What happens when you put a seed into dirt and give it water and light?** Allow children to respond. Say: **God gives seeds life so they can grow into plants. Look at the rest of the pictures on your sheet. Can someone tell me what is happening in these pictures?**

Give children time to share their ideas. Help children color the pictures and then cut along the lines to make four cards. Say: **Now mix your pictures up, and see if you can put them in order to show how the seed grows into a plant with a flower.**

After children have put their pictures in order a few times, have them set their pictures aside. Say: **God is amazing. He can take a little bitty seed and make a big, beautiful plant! We may water the plant and give it sunshine, but only God can give it life.**

3. Aquarium Sun-Catcher

Keep the scissors handy, and set out construction paper, glitter, and the starfish you prepared before class. Say: **Everywhere we go, we can find living things. Lots of God's animals and plants even live in the water. Can someone tell me a kind of plant or animal that lives in the ocean?** Encourage children to name several ocean animals or plants. You may need to remind the group about ocean life such as seaweed, starfish, or sea horses.

Say: **We're going to make pictures that look like oceans to remind us that God made all the life in the ocean.** Show children how to cut or tear sea creatures or plants out of the construction paper. While children work, take the backing off one circle of adhesive paper, and apply it to a paper plate with the center cut out. Make one paper plate for each child. Have the children place their creations on the sticky paper, and show them how to add glitter and starfish. When a child finishes, remove the backing from another adhesive circle, and use it to enclose the child's creation. Punch a hole in the rim of the plate, and string a piece of yarn through as a hanger. Have children set aside their sun catchers.

Life Is In the Bible

1. Breath Exploration

Have preschoolers gather around you. Hold up a doll, and say: **My**

Teacher Tip

You can enrich this activity by bringing in some seeds and a bedding plant such as a marigold. Let the children examine the seeds and the different parts of the plant, especially the roots.

Teacher Tip

If you have a seashell, bring it in, and pass it around for everyone to touch. Explain that seashells used to be animals that lived in the ocean.

doll's name is Mary. I like her very much. I can make her dance and wiggle. Move the doll around so the children can see. **I can even pretend that Mary is alive. But Mary is a doll, and no matter how hard I want her to be alive, she isn't. Animals and plants and people are alive. Only God can make living things.**

The Bible tells us that life is a gift from God. Open your Bible to Genesis 2:7, and read the verse aloud. Say: **Wow! God made a man with dirt and then breathed into the man to give him life. God is amazing! Only God can give life.**

God gave the first man breath. Things that are alive breathe. Blow on your hand. What does your breath feel like? Let's see what our breath can do.

Have children sit at tables. Give each child a cup, and then fill each cup halfway with water. Distribute straws, and have children blow into the water. Ask: **What does your breath do to the water?**

Say: **Living things breathe. God gave the first person breath, and he gives breath to you and me.**

Have children save their cups of water to drink during the snack.

2. Living Things Eat

Have the children wash their hands and then sit back down. Say: **God gave us life, and living things need food to eat and water to drink. The Bible tells us that God gave a special garden to the first people he made.** Hold up the Bible, and read aloud Genesis 2:8-9a. Say: **God gave you life and cares about you and me just as much as he cared about the first people. He gives us good food to eat, too.**

Pass around the fruit slices. As children eat, say: **All of this fruit came from living plants.**

● **What other foods come from plants?**

● **If you were going to make a garden, what plants would you put in it?**

Say: **God is very good to us because he loves us. He made us and gave us life, so he gives us food to live.**

3. Animals Don't Wear Pajamas

Move to an area where the children have room to stretch. Say: **I'm glad God gives us the food and water we need. He gives us something else we need to stay alive. There's a poem in the Bible that says, "[God] grants sleep to those he loves" (Psalm 127:2b). Did you know that you need sleep to live? All living things need rest. How does your body let you know you need rest?** Allow children to respond, and then say: **I know**

● ● ● ● ● ● ●

Teacher Tip

If you have time, blow into a balloon or across a pin-wheel so the children can see other effects of breath.

● ● ● ● ● ● ●

an action poem that will help us remember that all living things need rest. I'll say the words, and you help me do the actions. We'll practice, and then we'll do it again.

Gorillas don't wear pajamas (*shake your head "no"*),
But they gather up leaves in a pile. (*Pretend to push leaves in a pile.*)
They make a nice nest,
Lie down for a rest (*pretend to stretch and yawn*),
And forget about life for a while.

Sea otters don't wear pajamas (*shake your head "no"*);
They're warm in their thick, furry coats. (*Hug yourself.*)
They rest in seaweed (*throw your head back and your arms out*);
It's just what they need
To sleep while staying afloat.

Flowers don't wear pajamas (*shake your head "no"*),
But some of them close up at night. (*Bring your hands together over your head.*)
They wait for the sun (*look up*),
And when day's begun,
They open up wide toward the light. (*Bring your hands out to either side with palms up.*)

I wear pajamas (*nod your head "yes"*),
And I pull up my blanket just so. (*Pretend to grasp a blanket and pull.*)
I tightly close my eyes (*close your eyes*),
And then the time flies
'Til I get up, ready to go. (*Open your eyes and stretch.*)

After repeating the rhyme a few times, say: **All living things need to rest. God gave us life, and he made sure we'd get sleepy and rest sometimes, too.**

Let's Thank God for Life

1. Creature Prayer Song

Say: **Aren't you glad that God made all the wonderful, different living things and that he takes good care of them? I sure am! Let's thank God by singing him a song.**

Ask children to name three living things God made. Then sing the following song to the tune of "God Is So Good."

> **God made the** [living thing].
> **God made the** [living thing].
> **God made the** [living thing].
> **Thank you, thank you, God.**

Allow the children to suggest various creatures to sing the song several times. To end, sing the following verse:

> **God made me, too.**
> **God made me, too.**
> **God made me, too.**
> **Thank you, thank you, God.**

51

God Created Light

In the dark of night, lamplight comforts us. During early morning hours, the light of sunrise promises a new day. By the light of a cheery campfire, we feel safe and warm. Light balances the darkness, helps us find our way, energizes us, and stimulates health and growth. It's absolutely necessary for life. Light, in fact, is such a special gift from God that Jesus is called the light of our world (John 1:4).

Preschoolers love exploring light. They love to "catch" flashlight beams on walls, control light by playing with light switches, and watch the shapes and shadows light creates. Through this lesson, you can help your preschoolers learn that light is more than fun and games; light is a gift from God that guides us and helps us grow.

Supply List

- a Bible
- a flashlight with good batteries
- two medium-sized balloons
- two dark T-shirts
- a photocopy of the "Saul Figure" handout (p. 58) for each child
- crayons
- a wooden stick for each child (chopsticks work well)
- glue
- a large box (at least 18x24 inches)
- scissors
- white fabric or paper
- tape
- marshmallow creme
- chocolate cookies
- plastic knives
- napkins
- two medium-sized bowls

Preparation

To build a shadow box, lay the large box on its side so the top opens toward you. Cut out one end of the box, leaving at least a half-inch edge. Cut a piece of white fabric or paper to cover this hole, and tape it down. In the opposite end of the box, cut another hole to allow light from your light source to enter.

God Created Light

1. Flashlight Tag

Gather children around you, and ask:

● **Have you ever played Hide and Seek? What do you like best about playing Hide and Seek?**

● **What is it like to hide in the dark? in the light?**

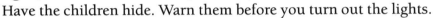

Say: **Today we're going to talk about the light God made. First let's see how light shines and helps us see when it's dark. I want each of you to find a place to hide. Then I'll turn off the lights and try to find you with my flashlight. If the light from my flashlight touches your face, follow the light, and come hold my hand.** Have the children hide. Warn them before you turn out the lights.

As you find each child, have him or her hold hands and walk around with you. After you've found all the children, turn on the lights, set aside the flashlight, and ask:

● **What was it like to hide in the dark?**

● **How did the light from my flashlight help?**

Say: **God made the light to help us see. The light from my flashlight helped me to see you even in the dark.**

2. Light and Dark

Lead the children outside to a sunny spot, and ask:

● **How does bright, sunny light feel on your face?**

Lead the children to a shady spot, and ask:

● **How does shady darkness feel on your face?**

Say: **A bright, sunny light makes us feel nice and warm. Do you think the light from the sun could make water warmer during our class time today?** Allow children to respond. **Let's find out. First I'll fill two balloons with water. Then I'll wrap one balloon in a dark T-shirt and set it in the sunshine. I'll wrap the other balloon in a dark T-shirt and leave it in a dark, shadowy place.** Fill the balloons, wrap them in T-shirts, and allow children to choose a sunny spot and a shady spot.

Teacher Tip

Make sure your room is dark enough to play this game. If necessary, place blankets, dark sheets, or trash bags over the windows.

Teacher Tip

Some preschoolers may be afraid of the dark and therefore reluctant to hide. Either allow these children to hide with partners, or have them hold your hand and help you seek others.

53

Teacher Tip

Don't completely
fill the balloons
with water.
Because heat
causes expansion,
the balloon in the
sun could burst if
you fill it
completely.

After you've placed the balloons, say: **Toward the end of our class time today, we'll come back to check our balloons. We'll see if the water in the sunny balloon is hotter than the water in the shady balloon.**

3. Light and Shadows

Say: **We're going to hear a story about light in the Bible, but first we need to make one of the people from the story.** Give each child a copy of the "Saul Figure" handout (p. 58). Set out crayons, and allow children to color their pictures. As children finish, help them cut out their pictures and glue each picture to a wooden stick to make a puppet.

Gather children around the shadow box, and shine your flashlight through the smaller hole so it hits the white screen. Then let children take turns putting their puppets into the shadow box to create shadows. Have one of the children in your class move a puppet closer to the light, and point out that the shadow gets bigger and bigger. Then have a volunteer move a puppet away from the light, and point out that the shadow gets smaller and smaller. Ask:

Teacher Tip

Quickly move into
the next activity,
but remember to
leave enough time
to come back to
this hands-on
demonstration of
the warming
impact of light.

● **What does the light do for us?**
● **Why do you think God made light?**

Say: **God made the light to help us see!** Turn off the flashlight. **Without the light, it's hard to see. I don't see the shadows anymore.** Turn on the flashlight. **When we have God's good light, we can see!**

Light Is in the Bible

1. Saul and the Bright Light

Say: **The Bible tells us many stories about light. In this story, Jesus really gets someone's attention with light.** Open your Bible to Acts 9:3-8, and show children the passage. Then select several volunteers to help you tell the story of Saul's encounter with Jesus. Tell one volunteer to listen carefully so he or she will know when to turn the flashlight on and off. Tell two other volunteers that they'll take turns using their Saul figures to act out the story by making shadows in the shadow box. Then tell the following story:

A long time ago, a man named Saul didn't like Jesus. He was very mean to the people who loved Jesus and even tried to hurt them. One day, Saul was walking down the road. Have a "Saul" volunteer "walk" the Saul figure in front of the box. **Jesus had a big surprise for Saul. He wanted to get Saul's attention. And do you know how Jesus got Saul's attention? With a very bright light!** Have your "light" volunteer turn on the flashlight and shine it into the shadow box. **Jesus sent such a bright**

light from heaven that it made Saul fall to the ground. Have the second "Saul" volunteer put a figure of Saul inside the shadow box and show him falling down. Ask:

- **How does it feel when the bright sun shines in our eyes?**
- **How do you think Saul's eyes felt in that bright light?**

Say: **Jesus' light sure got Saul's attention! Then Jesus said to Saul, "Saul, why are you doing bad things to the people who love me?" Saul couldn't believe it. He asked, "Who are you?" and Jesus answered, "I am Jesus." And do you know what? Instead of being mean to people who loved Jesus, Saul became their friend.** Have both "Saul" volunteers make their figures walk together and hug inside the shadow box. **In fact, Saul even began to love Jesus too.**

It sure is a good thing that God made the light! The light helps us to see, and the light helped Saul see Jesus.

Repeat the story to allow each child a chance to play Saul.

2. A "Light" Snack

Open your Bible to Psalm 18:28b, and show children the passage. Say: **Listen to what one man said about the light. "My God turns my darkness into light." God gives us light to help us! Let's make a snack together to think about how God gives us light.**

Set out the marshmallow creme, chocolate cookies, napkins, and plastic knives. Show children how to place a cookie on a napkin and spread some marshmallow creme on the cookie. Then hold up the cookie, and ask:

- **Which side is dark, and which is light?**

Hold the cookie side toward the children. Say: **Our Bible verse said God turns our darkness** (flip the cookie around so the marshmallow creme faces the children) **into light. God loves us, so he made the light for us.**

Help the children make their own snacks. Before children eat, say: **The bright marshmallow creme reminds us of the bright and sunny light God made. Let's thank God for making the light.** Pray: **Dear God, thank you for giving us light to help us see and grow and live. In Jesus' name, amen.**

3. This Little Light

Open your Bible to Ecclesiastes 11:7, and show the verse to the children. Say: **This verse tells us how good the light is. It says, "Light is sweet, and it pleases the eyes to see the sun." How many of you like to see the sun?** Allow children to respond. **Let's sing a song that talks about**

Teacher Tip

If you don't know this song, simply speak the words for children to repeat and do the motions.

the sweet, pleasing light of the sun. Explain that a sunbeam is the light from the sun. Have children form a circle to sing and do motions to "This Little Light of Mine."

This little light of mine (*hold your index finger up, and rotate it*)—
I'm gonna let it shine. (*Hold up your arm, and wave your index finger back and forth.*)
This little light of mine (*hold your index finger up, and rotate it*)—
I'm gonna let it shine. (*Hold up your arm, and wave your index finger back and forth.*)
This little light of mine (*hold your index finger up, and rotate it*)—
I'm gonna let it shine (*hold up your arm, and wave your index finger back and forth*),
Let it shine (*hold up your arm, and wave your index finger back and forth*),
Let it shine (*hold up your arm, and wave your index finger back and forth*),
Let it shine. (*Hold up your arm, and wave your index finger back and forth.*)
Hide it under a bushel? No! (*Cover index finger with other hand; then uncover index finger.*)
I'm gonna let it shine. (*Hold up your arm, and wave your index finger back and forth.*)
Hide it under a bushel? No! (*Cover index finger with other hand; then uncover index finger.*)
I'm gonna let it shine. (*Hold up your arm, and wave your index finger back and forth.*)
Hide it under a bushel? No! (*Cover index finger with other hand; then uncover index finger.*)
I'm gonna let it shine. (*Hold up your arm, and wave your index finger back and forth.*)
Let it shine (*hold up your arm, and wave your index finger back and forth*),
Let it shine (*hold up your arm, and wave your index finger back and forth*),
Let it shine. (*Hold up your arm, and wave your index finger back and forth.*)

After the song, say: **Now let's see how the sunbeams have warmed up the water in the balloons!**

Return to the water balloons wrapped in dark T-shirts, and pour the water from the balloons into the two bowls. Let the children feel the water in both bowls; then ask:

● **Which water feels warmer to you?**
● **How did the water warm up?**
● **How does the light from the sun warm you up?**

Say: **God loves us, so he made light for us. The light helps us to see,** and it warms us up just as it warmed up the water in these balloons. I'm glad God made the light, aren't you? Let's thank God for making light for us.

Let's Thank God for Light

1. Action Prayer

Have the children stand in a circle again and join you in the following action prayer to thank God for light.

> **Thank you, God, for making light.** (*Raise your hands on "thank you," and spread your arms wide on "light."*)
>
> **Thank you, God, for giving sight.** (*Raise your hands on "thank you," and point to your eyes on "sight."*)
>
> **Thank you, God, for light we see.** (*Raise you hands on "thank you," and then point to the sun.*)
>
> **Thank you, God, for loving me.** (*Raise your hands on "thank you," and point to yourself on "me."*)

God Created the Oceans

On the third day of Creation, God blessed his amazing world with the beauty of oceans. On the fifth day, God filled the oceans with an amazing variety of life. From God's oceans we receive pleasure and enjoyment, food, energy, minerals, medicines, and other gifts. Through oceans, God provides for our aesthetic, social, and physical needs.

What preschooler is not enthralled with beach sand, seashells, crabs, and seaweed? Preschoolers who visit the seashore are awed by the sprays of salty foam, waves crashing against rocks, and the rhythmic movement of ocean water. By leading your preschoolers to explore oceans, you can teach them the many ways God provides for his people.

Supply List

- a Bible
- a shoe-box lid or similar cardboard piece for each child
- blue and tan or brown modeling dough
- a bowl of clean sand
- graham cracker bears or gummy bear candies
- a container of strong saltwater
- a container of tap water
- several objects that float and several that sink—a cork, bark, a plastic ball, a solid rock, a metal spoon, and a plum, for example
- slices of bread
- plastic knives
- olives
- prepared tuna salad
- napkins

Preparation

For each child, cut a slice of bread to resemble a fish body. (See the illustration on page 63.) On each slice of bread, make the fish's "mouth" by cutting out a small triangle about one and a half inches above the bottom on the left-hand side.

Use another slice of bread to cut six "tails." Cut off the four corners of the bread, forming four triangles and leaving a diamond shape. Then cut the diamond shape into two additional triangles. You'll need one triangle "tail" for each child. Also slice olives into thin, round pieces.

God Created the Oceans

1. Swimming Sea Creatures

Gather children around you, and ask:

● **How many of you have been to the ocean? an aquarium?**

● **Can you tell me something you saw while you were there?**

● **What are things that live in the ocean that we might not get to see when we're there?**

● **How do you think all those creatures got into the ocean?**

Say: **God made the ocean, and he made everything in the ocean. God really gave us something special when he made the oceans.**

Say: **We're going to pretend we're some of the wonderful creatures God put into the ocean. Let's use our hands to be octopuses.** Show children how to wave their arms up and down like an octopus's tentacles. Then say: **The biggest animals in the ocean are called whales. Sometimes whales like to jump up out of the water and splash back down. Let's pretend to be whales.** Encourage children to jump up and make sounds like big splashes of water. Next say: **If you've ever seen crabs at the ocean, you know how funny they look when they walk. Let's all get down on the floor and walk like crabs.** Show children how to crab-walk. Then ask for volunteers to think of other ocean creatures and show everyone how to act them out.

After a few minutes, say: **God made many wonderful animals that live in the ocean, didn't he? Let's have some more fun learning about the ocean God made.**

2. Let's Go to the Beach!

Ask:

● **What do people like to do when they go to the beach?**

Help the children name things like build sand castles, swim, fish, and find seashells. Say: **God gave us a really neat playground when he made the oceans, didn't he? Let's make ocean pictures to show the fun things we can do at the beach.**

Set out the shoe-box lids, modeling dough, bowl of sand, and graham cracker bears or gummy bear candies.

Have each child spread tan or brown modeling dough in the bottom half of a shoe-box lid. Then have children lightly sprinkle sand on top of the dough and press it lightly so it will stay in place. Next, have each child spread blue modeling dough in the top half of the lid. Finally, encourage children to use the bear crackers or gummy bear candies to create beach scenes. As preschoolers work, ask:

● **What fun things are your bears doing at the ocean?**

● **Why do you think God made the oceans?**

Say: **God made the oceans, and he wants us to enjoy them. Next let's think about the water at the ocean.**

Have children set aside their ocean pictures.

3. Floating in Ocean Water

Set out the container of saltwater, the container of tap water, and the objects that float or sink. Say: **The ocean's water is salty. Why do you think God made the oceans salty?** Allow children to respond. **God made oceans with salty water and filled them with plants and animals that need the salt to live. The salt helps things to float better!** Point out the containers of saltwater and tap water. Allow the children to take turns placing various objects in the tap water and the saltwater to determine which things will float in one but not in the other. As preschoolers experiment, continue to remind them which water is salty and which isn't.

After everyone has had a turn, set aside the objects and the water. Ask:

● **Which kind of water helps things float better?**

● **Why do you think God put salt in the water?**

Say: **God loves us and likes to help us out. He made the oceans and filled them with plants and animals. To help those animals live better, he put salt in the oceans. God is so good to everything he makes!**

Oceans Are in the Bible

1. God's Wonderful Ocean

Open your Bible to Jeremiah, and show it to the children. Say: **In the book of Jeremiah in the Bible, God talks about the oceans.** Read aloud Jeremiah 5:22b, and say: **God is telling us that he made the oceans just right. The water and the sand and the waves—they are all here because God made them. Stand with me in a circle so we can pretend to be an ocean.**

Have children form a circle and hold hands. Say: **Now, let's add waves to our ocean.** Show children how to move their arms up and down to create a wavy circle. Say: **Now we need to add some ocean animals to our**

· · · · · · · ·

Teacher Tip

You may want to test this activity beforehand. The salt content should be fairly high; some objects will demonstrate the difference better than others.

· · · · · · · ·

ocean. Have children take turns being sea animals, such as flying fish, sharks, whales, or eels. Allow children to "swim" inside the circle as the other children continue to make waves. Then have the children sit down. Ask:

● **What's your favorite ocean animal?**

● **Why do you think God put so many different animals in the ocean?**

Say: **God knew that the world would need lots of different animals and plants, so he made oceans and put lots of things in them.**

Teacher Tip

If time permits, you can also turn this activity into a dramatic presentation. Choose five children to come to the front of the room. Number the children, and remind them what "shark number one" says, "shark number two" says, and so on. Then have the whole class say the rhyme, but have the "sharks" say their lines alone.

2. Super-Special Sea Creatures

Open your Bible to Psalm 95, and show it to the children. **Say: Psalm 95:5a says, "The sea is [God's], for he made it." God made the oceans. We're going to learn a finger play to help us remember that God made the oceans and put wonderful creatures in it. It goes like this:**

Five little sharks, swimming in the sea. (*Hold up five fingers and wiggle them.*)

The first shark said, "Now come and follow me." (*Hold up one finger, and then motion to "come here."*)

The second shark said, "The water sure is fun." (*Hold up two fingers, and then clap.*)

The third shark said, "I like swimming in the sun." (*Hold up three fingers, and then form a circle with your arms as the sun.*)

The fourth shark asked, "Who made the sea for you and me?" (*Hold up four fingers, and then shrug shoulders with hands in the air.*)

The fifth shark said, "God made the sea!" (*Hold up five fingers, and then point up.*)

Do the finger play several times with different ocean animals.

3. Fishy Snacks

Set out the precut bread slices (two bodies with tails for each child), tuna fish salad, olive slices, plastic knives, and napkins.

Open a Bible to John 21:1-13, and show children the page. Say: **In the Bible we can read about Jesus' friends. They were in a boat on the sea, trying to catch some fish to eat. They had fished all night long but hadn't caught a single fish! They were tired and sad and hungry. Can you show me your tired, sad, and hungry faces?** Pause for children to respond. **Oh, you look so tired and sad and hungry! Jesus' friends just kept trying. Then they saw a man on the beach. The man said they should catch**

fish from the other side of the boat. They tried it, and do you know what happened? They caught so many fish that they couldn't even carry them all! Wow! That's a lot of fish! I bet Jesus' friends were surprised and happy. Can you show me your best surprised and happy faces? Pause for children to respond. **Oh, you look so happy! Jesus' friends wanted to thank the man, so they took their boat back to the beach. Do you know who the man on the beach was? Jesus! Jesus helped his friends catch fish from the sea so they could eat. And that's just what they did. I think it's time for us to eat a little bit of fish from the sea, too!**

Distribute napkins, and show children how to arrange their bread slices on the napkins. Help children make sandwiches by helping them put a little tuna salad on their bread slices and add olive slices as eyes.

Before eating, pray: **Dear God, thank you for making the beautiful ocean and the fish for us to eat.** Then call on each child to give thanks for something special about the ocean. This can be as simple as, "Thank you for fish."

Let's Thank God for the Oceans

1. Thank You, God, for the Ocean Blue

Say: **We're going to learn a singing prayer of thanksgiving to thank God for making the beautiful oceans.** Sing the following singing prayer to the tune of "Frèrè Jacques," and lead children in acting out the motions.

Thank you, God, for your great oceans (*make prayer hands*),
Fish and whales, dolphins too (*keep hands together and "swim" them back and forth*),
Octopus and starfish (*wiggle all fingers*),
Jellyfish and sharks. (*On "sharks," show teeth.*)
Thank you for the ocean blue! (*Make prayer hands.*)

Thank you, God, for your great oceans (*make prayer hands*),
Salty seas, waves that splash (*move arms like waves*),
Sand and shells and breezes (*move hands back and forth on "breezes"*),
Lots of fun to visit. (*Nod head and give a thumbs-up sign.*)
Thank you for the ocean blue! (*Make prayer hands.*)

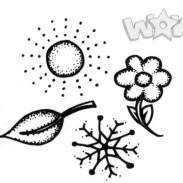

God Created the Seasons

The four seasons proclaim God's creativity, faithfulness, and provision. The cold, frosty winter allows the earth to rest. The cool and rainy spring renews the earth for summer. The warm summer promotes growth. The cool, crisp fall provides a plentiful harvest. Each season has unique characteristics and much-needed benefits, so God gives us the seasons in a consistent pattern we can count on.

Preschoolers are sensory learners. As they learn about the seasons, children will use their five senses to explore the world God created. They'll delight in the changing seasons and understand that God provides a planned order to the seasons. Use this lesson to reassure children that just as the seasons are always the same, God, too, is always the same.

Supply List

- a Bible
- an ice pack
- a fresh flower
- a hot water bottle
- water
- a dry leaf
- an assortment of gloves, mittens, scarves, and hats so each child can have one
- straws
- colorful construction paper
- paper clips
- perfume
- two bags of lightweight, nonperishable groceries
- small cups
- pitcher of lemonade
- newsprint
- napkins
- plastic knives
- rice cakes
- marshmallow creme
- sliced strawberries
- sliced bananas
- a bowl of cereal flakes

Teacher Tip

You may want to sprinkle some lemon juice over the bananas to prevent browning.

Preparation

Just before class, fill the hot water bottle with warm water. Hide the gloves, mittens, scarves, and hats around the room.

God Created the Seasons

1. The Four Seasons

Set out the ice pack, the flower, the hot water bottle, and the leaf.

Gather children around, and say: **Today we're going to talk about the seasons. God made four seasons: winter, spring, summer, and fall.** Ask:

● **How do we know it's winter? spring? summer? fall?**

Say: **God made every season different, didn't he? We may like to play in the snow in winter, but we can't play in the snow in summer. It doesn't snow in summer.**

Pick up the ice pack, and say: **Oh, this is very cold! This makes me think about winter. What things do we do or see in winter? Let's pass around this ice pack and each tell one thing we do or see in winter.** If children have trouble, help them name such things as snow, icicles, and hot chocolate. When the ice pack comes back to you, set it aside. Then pick up the fresh flower. Smell the flower, and say: **Ahh, this flower makes me think about spring. Lots of pretty flowers like this one grow during the spring.** Pass the flower around, and encourage each child to touch and smell the flower. When the flower comes back to you, set it aside. Then pick up the hot water bottle, and say: **Wow, this is hot! This makes me think about summer because it's so hot during the summer. What things do we do or see in summer? Let's pass around this hot water bottle and each tell one thing we do or see in summer.** If children have trouble, help them name such things as sun, swimming pools, and lemonade. When the hot water bottle comes back to you, set it aside. Then pick up the dry leaf, and say: **This dry leaf makes me think of fall. In the fall, lots of leaves like this turn pretty colors and fall off the trees.** Pass around the leaf so each child has a chance to touch it. When it comes back to you, set it aside. Ask:

● **What season do you like best—winter, spring, summer or fall—and why?**

● **Why do you think God made four different seasons?**

Say: **All the seasons are different, and we need each one of them. God loves us, and he gives us everything we need. That's why he made four seasons. Let's look a little more closely now at each season.**

2. Winter

Have children sit in a circle. Say: **God made four seasons. Winter is one of them. We're going to do an action rhyme about a snowman who** lost his warm winter clothes. I'll say the rhyme, and we'll do the motions together.

> **Once a little snowman went outside to play.** *(Pretend to open a door.)*
> **A hat, a scarf, and mittens were what he wore that day.** *(Touch your head, your neck, and your hand.)*
> **But as he stood there playing, a sudden gust of air** *(wave your hands back and forth as wind)*
> **Blew his hat right off his head and left it cold and bare!** *(Touch your head with both your hands.)*
> **The snowman's head was chilly, but still he didn't go.** *(Hug yourself and shiver.)*
> **Then the snowman's mittens fell deep into the snow.** *(Hold your hands up.)*
> **He stayed outside to play, though very cold was he.** *(Hug yourself and shiver.)*
> **Then the snowman's scarf got caught on a frozen tree.** *(Touch your neck with both hands.)*
> **Poor little snowman. Where did his clothing go?** *(Shrug your shoulders.)*
> **Unless we help him find his clothes, he'll play in no more snow.** *(Shake your index finger "no.")*

Say: **We're going to try to help the snowman who lost his winter clothes. Walk around the room, and try to find one piece of the snowman's winter clothes. Find one thing, and then come back and sit with me again.**

When everyone is seated again, say: **Now put on the winter clothes you found, and we'll sing a song. I'll sing a line and do a motion, and then you sing back to me and do the motion.**

Give children a moment to put on their winter clothes. Then sing this song to the tune of "Frosty the Snowman."

> **Hey, little snowman** *(wave "hello"),*
> **We found your winter clothes.** *(Hold up the winter clothing you're wearing.)*
> **Now you can go outside to play** *(point toward the window)*
> **On this cold winter's day.** *(Hug yourself and shiver.)*

Say: **God made all the seasons, and he made winter very cold and snowy. In the winter, we need our warm winter clothes to keep us**

Teacher Tip

Preschoolers are just beginning to understand opposites, so they may recognize summer and winter more readily than spring or fall. You can help them by naming things that typically happen in each season, such as snow for winter, flowers for spring, heat for summer, and falling leaves for fall.

warm. Next let's talk about the season that comes after winter.

Collect the winter clothing from children, and set it aside.

3. Spring

Set out straws, paper clips, and construction paper.

Say: **Spring is the season that comes right after winter. In the spring, the snow melts, and beautiful things like flowers grow. To celebrate that a beautiful spring comes after the winter, we're going to make spring flowers.**

Have preschoolers tear flower shapes out of the construction paper. Then show children how to attach a flower to a straw with a paper clip. Finally, spray a little perfume on each child's flower.

Say: **After the cold and snow of winter, God made lots of beautiful flowers in the spring for us to enjoy. Now let's find out what season comes after spring.**

Seasons Are in the Bible

1. Summer

Say: **Summer comes right after spring. Can you think of some things you like to do in the summer?** Allow children to respond. **We like to have a lot of fun in the summer, don't we? Well, the Bible talks about some things we need to do in the summer.**

Open your Bible to Proverbs 10:5, and show the page to the children. Then read the verse aloud. Say: **This verse says that summer is made for collecting food. God made the summer sunny and warm so food would grow. Food that grows in the summer feeds us in the winter. God made the seasons in just the right way. Let's pretend that it's summer and that we're collecting food so we'll have something to eat in the winter.**

Have the children form two teams and stand in single-file lines that stretch across the room. At one end, place a bag of groceries next to each team. Say: **We need to collect all this food that we've grown in the warm, sunny summer. We need to save it to eat during the cold, snowy winter.** Explain that each team will need to pass the items in its bag down the line until they get to the other side of the room. Encourage the children to pretend that they're hot and sweaty in the summer sun as they pass their food items.

When everyone understands how to play, have the children begin. When children have passed all the food items to the other side of the room, say: **You did a wonderful job collecting food! Aren't you hot and sweaty now from working so hard in the summer sun? Now enjoy a cool treat after your hard work.**

Serve lemonade to the children. As they drink, ask:
- **Why do you think God made summer?**
- **Why do you think God put summer after spring and before fall and winter?**

Say: **God's world needs every season to work just right. God put the seasons in exactly the right order. Now let's learn about the fourth season.**

2. Fall

Say: **Fall comes right after summer. Summer is hot and sunny, but God doesn't want us to get too hot! So God made the fall cooler. In the fall, the leaves begin to change colors, and people rake the leaves in big piles.**

Trees need to grow new leaves to be healthy. But first, trees have to lose their old leaves in the fall. That's the way God made it.

Pass out large pieces of newsprint to the children. Ask the children to crumple up their paper and listen to the noise the paper makes.

Say: **The sound of crumpling paper makes me think of walking on crunchy leaves in the fall. Let's pretend to rake our "leaves" into a big pile.**

Ask the children to "rake" their paper balls into a big pile in the center of the room. Then have the children line up and take turns rolling in the pile of paper leaves. Finally, have the children "rake" the leaves and put them into the trash can or recycling box. Ask:
- **What other things do we do during the fall?**
- **Why do you think God made fall a chilly season?**

Say: **Fall is a fun season. God made fall, the leaves, the cool weather, and windy days. That's the way fall is every year.**

Open your Bible to Jeremiah 5:24b, and read the Scripture aloud. Then say: **God made all the seasons at just the right time, and he knew what the world needed during each season.**

3. Every Season

Say: **Winter, spring, summer, and fall happen in the same order and at just the right time every year. A very smart man wrote in the Bible about the seasons. He wrote, "There is a time for everything, and a season for** every activity under heaven" (Ecclesiastes 3:1). **Let's make a snack to remind us that the seasons are in the same order every year.**

Have children wash their hands as you set out napkins, plastic knives, rice cakes, marshmallow creme, sliced strawberries, sliced bananas, and a bowl of cereal.

Distribute a napkin and a rice cake to each child. Then show children how to spread some marshmallow creme on one quarter of the rice cake as snow. Next to the marshmallow creme, have children put a strawberry slice as a flower, then a banana slice as the summer sun, and finally a few cereal flakes as fall leaves. Show children how their snack wheels keep going round and round in the same order just as the seasons happen in the same order every year.

As children eat, say: **God loves us and knows what we need, so he made the four seasons to make sure we have what we need. Let's thank God for giving us four seasons.**

Let's Thank God for the Seasons

1. Action Prayer

Say: **We've learned that God made the seasons for us. We've also learned that the seasons come in a special order every year. We can count on the seasons to come in that order. We can count on God, too, all year long. Let's thank God for making the seasons by doing an action prayer.** Have the children think of motions to do for winter, spring, summer, and fall. For winter, children could hug themselves and shiver. For spring, they could crouch down on the ground like seeds and then pop up like flowers. For summer, they could fan their faces as if they're hot. For fall, they could pretend to rake leaves.

Tell the children they'll need to do the motions as you call out the seasons. Then pray: **Dear God, we thank you for the cold and snowy winter.** Pause. **We thank you for the fresh and flowery spring.** Pause. **We thank you for the hot and sunny summer.** Pause. **We thank you for the cool and leafy fall. Thank you for loving us so much that you made all the seasons just right. Amen.**

God Created Space

"How does our world hang in the sky?" "Will it ever fall?" "Why are stars so teeny-tiny, and why do they twinkle?" "Why does the moon look skinny sometimes and round sometimes?"

Young children bubble over with questions about their universe. Three-, four-, and five-year-olds don't want to just hear about the stars; they want to reach up and grab them! They want to taste space and zoom around in it. But space can also make preschoolers feel very small and insignificant. They may wonder, "Does God notice me down here?"

This lesson will launch your budding astronomers on a mission to discover who made our amazing universe. This lesson will help children learn that, although they sometimes feel small, God made everything and loves them most of all.

Supply List

- a Bible
- "Planets" illustration (p. 77)
- white paper
- glow-in-the-dark crayons
- tape
- glow-in-the-dark stars
- scissors
- a flashlight
- sugar cookie dough (one package for every ten children)
- an oven
- wax paper
- cookie sheets
- newspaper
- paper lunch bags
- glitter
- pillows
- blankets or sleeping bags
- taped instrumental music
- cassette player
- napkins
- a variety of cookie decorations—tubes of icing, candies, candy sprinkles, and cereal, for example
- a pencil
- a ball
- glue

Preparation

Using the "Planets" illustration (p. 77) as a guide, sketch each planet and the sun and color them with glow-in-the-dark crayons. Then hang the planets around the room and the glow-in-the-dark stars in one corner.

● ● ● ● ● ● ● ●

Teacher Tip

For an extra splash, paint your planets with fluorescent fabric paint. This paint, which you can find at most fabric stores, is permanent and takes at least four hours to dry.

● ● ● ● ● ● ● ●

About fifteen minutes before class, take the sugar cookie dough out of the refrigerator to let it soften.

Also, cut a star out of white paper for each child. (See pattern below.)

God Created Space

1. Mission Exploration

Gather the children together, and ask:

● **When it's dark outside, what do you see in the sky?**

Say: **We see the stars and the moon when it's dark outside. We can also see planets. We live on a planet called Earth. God made other planets, too. Would you like to go with me to see some of the other planets far away?** Allow children to respond. **Let's pretend to visit each planet as I tell you about them. I'm going to turn the lights down.**

Turn the lights down, and turn on the flashlight. Lead children to the sun. Say: **The sun isn't a planet. It is a star. God made the sun a huge, super-hot ball of fire. The middle of the sun is more than 25 million degrees. Wow! That's very hot!**

Lead children to Mercury, and say: **This planet is called Mercury. Can you say that?** Pause. **God made Mercury and put it closer to the sun than any other planet. The side of Mercury that faces the sun is very hot—hotter than anything on earth. But the side that doesn't face the sun is freezing cold—colder than anything on Earth. No people, animals, or plants can live on Mercury.**

Lead children to Venus, and say: **We call this planet Venus. Can you say that?** Pause. **Venus is the planet nearest to us. Very thick clouds**

● ● ● ● ● ● ● ●

Teacher Tip

The glow-in-the-dark crayons or paints show best if the room is very dark. However, some preschoolers may be frightened of the dark. Have the children hold hands if they'd like, or ask adult volunteers to hold hands with children who are afraid.

● ● ● ● ● ● ● ●

cover Venus, and it's very, very hot. We couldn't live on Venus, either.

Lead children to Earth, and say: **Of course, Earth is our very own home. Our planet is the only one with trees, people, water, or food. God knew just where to put the earth. If the earth were a little closer to the sun, we'd melt. If it were farther away, we'd freeze. God is very wise, isn't he?**

Lead children to Mars, and say: **This is Mars. Mars is called the red planet because it's covered with red dirt. There is a lot of dust and wind on Mars, but nothing lives there.**

Lead children to Jupiter, and say: **We call this planet Jupiter. Can you say that?** Pause. **Jupiter is the biggest planet in our group of planets. Jupiter is just a ball of chemicals. Jupiter has a huge red spot that's actually a storm bigger than all of Earth! Jupiter may be fun to look at, but we couldn't live there.**

Lead kids to Saturn, and say: **We call this planet Saturn. Can you say that?** Pause. **When God made Saturn, he dressed it up in a special way. God gave Saturn beautiful rings. Those shiny rings are really dust and icy rocks. Some of the rocks are as big as your house!**

Lead children to Uranus, and say: **This it Uranus. Can you say that?** Pause. **Uranus is covered in thick fog and has rings around it as Saturn does. You wouldn't want to go to Uranus. It's super cold and very windy.**

Lead children to Neptune, and say: **This is Neptune. Can you say that?** Pause. **Neptune, like Jupiter, has a big spot that is actually a horrible storm as big as our whole Earth! Neptune's winds are the strongest of any planet. No one could live on Neptune.**

Lead children to Pluto, and say: **This is little Pluto. Can you say that?** Pause. **Pluto is the littlest planet and the farthest away from the sun. Pluto is really like a small ball of ice. We don't know very much about Pluto because it's so far away. God knows everything about Pluto, though, because he made it.**

Turn on the lights, and have children sit down. Ask:

● **What is your favorite planet?**

● **Why do you think God put people on earth?**

Say: **God knew earth was the perfect place to put us. It's just the right distance from the sun. God made everything on earth, and God made everything in space, too.**

2. Making Planet Cookies

Say: **I sure am hungry after our long trip around the universe. Let's make a snack to remind us of all the beautiful planets God made in space.**

Have the children wash their hands. Give children each a square of wax paper and a handful of cookie dough, and let them pound the dough into planets. While they're busy working, ask:

● **If you were really making your own planet, what would it be like?**

Say: **It's fun to make new things. I think God must have had a lot of fun when he made everything in space!**

When children have finished making their planet cookies, put them on cookie sheets, and bake them. While the cookies are in the oven, the children can do the next activity.

3. Star Makers

Seat the children at the table, and ask:

● **Where do you think the stars go in the daytime?**

Say: **The stars don't go away during the day. They're still there; we just can't see them. The sun is so bright that we just can't see any other light, including the light from the stars. Did you know that the sun is really a star?** Allow children to respond. Then ask:

● **How many stars do you think there are?**

Say: **There are millions and millions of stars. Only God knows how many stars there are. Let's make our very own star puppets.**

Spread newspaper on a table. Give each child a paper star to color with glow-in-the-dark crayons. The harder children press, the better their stars will glow in the dark. Have children glue the stars to the bottom of paper bags and then add glitter to their bags.

Turn off the lights to allow children to see their stars in the dark. Then turn the lights on again. Say: **God made everything in space. That tells us how powerful God is. But God knows you and loves you most of all!**

Have children set aside the star puppets to use later.

Space Is in the Bible

1. A Shepherd Boy Looks at the Sky

Set the pillows and blankets out under the stars you put up before class. Turn on the quiet music, and invite children to snuggle on the blankets or sleeping bags.

Say: **A very long time ago, a young boy named David worked in a field at night. It was very quiet. David could hear the wind blowing through the branches; he could hear the night bugs chirping; he could see the stars. David thought a lot about God. David wrote poems and songs, and we can read them in the book of Psalms in the Bible. Let's listen to some of David's poems and songs while we look at the stars.**

Turn off the lights, turn on the flashlight, and join the children under the stars to read the following interpretation.

God, you made everything so beautiful! When I look up into the night skies and see the work of your fingers—the moon and the stars you have created—I am amazed. The stars throw out their light into the sky, and I will praise you with all my heart (Psalm 9:1-2). **You created the planets and the entire universe out of nothing. You just said, "Let there be lights in the sky," and it happened** (Genesis 1:14).

When I think about how big the world is, I remember how little I am. But you think I'm important! You even put a crown on my head. You are amazing, God, and I love you (Psalm 8:3-5). Ask:

- **Why do you think David wrote these songs and poems?**
- **What do the stars and the moon make you think about God?**

Say: **God is so wonderful and wise that he made everything in space. But God also knows what's happening to each of us.**

2. Orbit Around Jesus

Ask: **Where does the sun go at night?**

Say: **The sun doesn't go away. We just can't see it because we're turned away from it.** Have all the children stand up in rows, facing you. Say: **Let's pretend that I'm the sun and you're the earth. Our earth turns slow circles, so why don't you turn slow circles, too?** As children are turning, ask: **Can you always see me, the sun?** Have children face away from you. Ask: **Has the sun gone away?**

Have children face you again and sit down. Say: **The sun hasn't gone away! Just as you couldn't always see me because you were turning, we can't always see the sun because our earth is turning. But God can always see the sun, and he can always see you! God has a perfect plan for the planets. God makes his planets follow a special circle so they won't hit each other.**

Have the children stand and form a circle to be the planets. Ask one child to be the sun and stand in the middle of the circle. Have the child in the middle of the circle stand still while all the other children slowly walk in a circle around him or her.

Say: **Just as you're circling around the "sun," the planets circle around the real sun. This way, the planets don't get in each other's way.**

Have the children sit down. Hold up a Bible, and say: **The Bible says that Jesus is the one who holds all things together** (Colossians 1:17). Ask:

- **What does it make you think about God that he can keep all these planets going just right?**

Say: **God is so very wonderful! Let's eat our planet cookies now to** remember how powerful God is to keep the planets going just the right way.

Distribute napkins, and set out the cookie decorations. Let the children decorate their planets and then gobble them up! Then have children wash their hands.

3. Calling Out the Stars

Gather children around you, and read this verse, which is adapted from Psalm 19:1-4: **The stars shout that God is amazing. They have no mouths, but the stars tell stories all day and night. Their words go out into all the earth.** Ask:

● **What do you think the stars say about God?**

● **What would you say to all the people on earth if you were a star?**

Say: **God knows everything about everything he made. It's as if God knows every star by name. We're going to name our star puppets, too.**

Have children find their star puppets again. Ask each child to name his or her star; then write the star's name on the puppet. Also write the child's name and the star's name on a piece of paper. Ask the children to remember the names they gave their stars.

Have the children place their puppets around the room. Turn off the lights so children can see all their stars twinkling. Then turn on the lights again, and explain that you're going to call each star by name. When you do, children can find their puppets again.

When everyone has a puppet again, ask:

● **If God cares about the stars, how do you think he feels about you?**

Say: **God made all the planets and the stars, and they're really neat! God knows all about space, and he loves you and knows all about you, too.**

Let's Thank God for Space

1. Orbit Prayer

Have children sit in a circle, and say: **When God made the earth, he made it just right for us to live in! Let's thank God for making Earth so special.** Hold up a ball. **Let's pretend that this ball is the earth. I'm going to pass it around the circle. When the ball gets to you, say thank you to God for one thing he made. Then pass the ball to the person next to you. I'll start. Dear God, thank you for the beautiful stars.** Pass the ball around the circle. Then close by praying: **Thank you, God, for making everything just right. Thank you for loving us so much that even though space is very big, you love each one of us.**

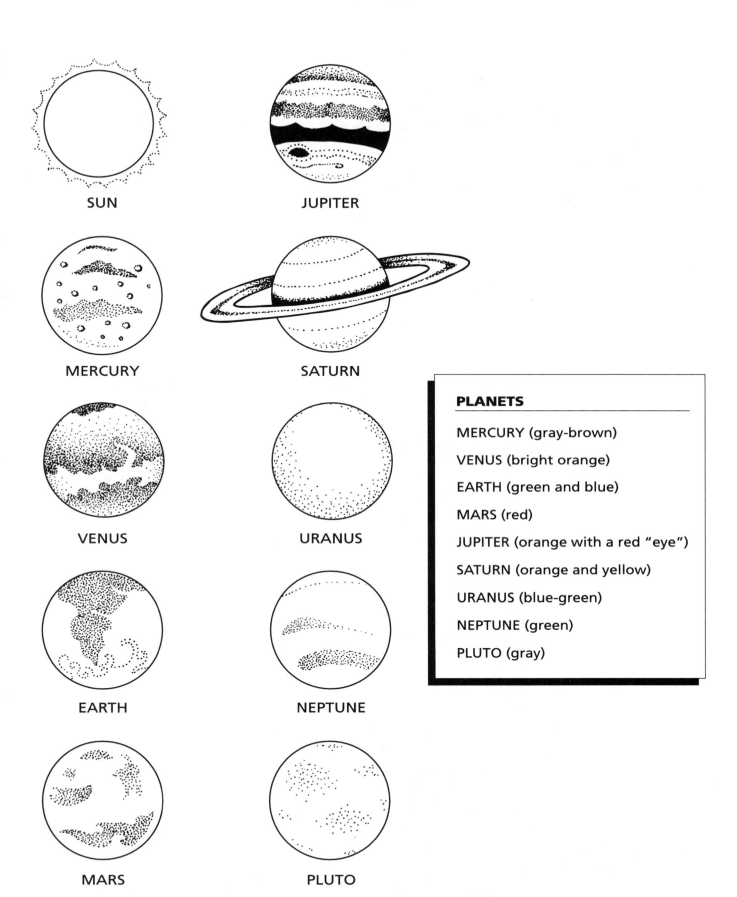

SUN

JUPITER

MERCURY

SATURN

VENUS

URANUS

EARTH

NEPTUNE

MARS

PLUTO

PLANETS

MERCURY (gray-brown)

VENUS (bright orange)

EARTH (green and blue)

MARS (red)

JUPITER (orange with a red "eye")

SATURN (orange and yellow)

URANUS (blue-green)

NEPTUNE (green)

PLUTO (gray)

God Created Water

Imagine jumping into a swimming pool on a hot day or satisfying your thirst with a cool glass of water. How many times every day do we turn to water to keep us healthy and make us feel better? We need water to survive, so God provides water. As a bonus, God made the water enjoyable. Water feels good, tastes good, looks good, sounds good, and even smells good.

Preschoolers know all about the joys of water. They love to play in the rain and splash in puddles. When they're thirsty, they drink. What young children probably don't realize is how important water is to life. As they learn about water, children will discover how interconnected they are with the world. Even more importantly, they'll discover how interconnected the world is with God. Use this lesson to show children how God provides water for their needs.

Supply List

- a Bible
- a dishpan of water
- spoons
- a bowl of ice cubes
- paper towels
- a cold-mist humidifier
- a hand mirror
- bowls of fresh and dried fruit, such as bananas and banana chips, apples and dried apples, plums and prunes, and peaches and dried peaches
- a cup of seeds and a plant
- scissors

- one small paper plate for each child
- newspaper
- crayons or water-based markers
- blue curling ribbon
- a large plastic cup
- a lightweight bucket with five feet of string attached to it
- white paper
- fruit stickers and heart stickers

Preparation

Set up three stations in the classroom. The first should have a dish pan of water, several spoons, and paper towels; the second should have a bowl of ice cubes; the third should have a humidifier and a hand mirror.

The humidifier should be plugged in, turned on, and humidifying as class begins.

For each child, cut a six-inch piece of curling ribbon, and place the ribbons in a large plastic cup.

For each child, cut a flower out of a small paper plate. To cut the flowers, stack three or four plates together, and then draw a circle in the center of the top plate. Cut five or six pie-shaped pieces into the plates, with the point of each pie piece stopping at the line of the center circle. Draw the center circle on each plate. Repeat the process until you have one flower for each child.

God Created Water

1. Different Kinds of Water

Gather children around you, and say: **Today we're going to learn about water. There are three ways that water looks and feels. Even though it looks and feels different, it's still water.** Lead children to the dishpan of water, and say: **Here is the first way we know water.** Ask:
- **How does the water feel?**
- **How do people use water?**

Allow the children to put their hands in the water and to use spoons to stir the water and drip the water. After a few minutes of play, have children dry their hands on paper towels. Then move to the bowl of ice, taking the paper towels with you. Say: **Here is the second way we know water.** Ask:
- **How does the ice feel?**
- **How do people use ice?**

Allow children to pick up ice cubes, bang them together, and suck on them. After a few minutes of play, have children dry their hands on paper towels. Then move to the humidifier, taking the paper towels with you. Say: **Here is the third way we know water.** Ask:
- **How does the steam feel?**
- **How do people use steam?**

Allow children to feel the steam with their hands. Hold up the mirror in front of the steam so children can see the condensation. After a few minutes of play, have the children dry their hands and then sit down. Ask:
- **Why do you think God made all of those kinds of water?**
- **Why is water good?**

Say: **Water helps us when we're thirsty. Ice keeps things cool. Steam can make dry things wet. God made water to help us.**

Teacher Tip

Although the humidifier doesn't actually emit steam, it's safer for preschoolers than hot steam.

Provide more fresh fruit than dried fruit. Most preschoolers will choose fresh fruit over dried fruit, and eating too much dried fruit can cause a tummy ache.

You may want to slice the fresh fruit just before class. To keep the fruit fresh, you can soak apple slices in lemon lime soda, or keep the skin on banana slices.

● ● ● ● ● ● ● ●

2. Water in Fruit

Have children wash their hands as you set out paper towels and the fresh and dried fruit. Then have children gather around the fruit. Say: **Look at this fruit. Taste it, smell it, and touch it to see how it's different.**

Give children a few minutes to eat. Remind them to observe the differences between the fresh fruit and dried fruit. Then ask:

● **How did the fresh fruit feel different from the dried fruit? smell different? taste different? look different?**

● **What do you think makes the fruit different?**

Say: **Water is inside the food we eat. Today we ate some fruit that had water in it and some fruit that had its water taken out.** Have the children guess which fruit had water in it and which had water taken out. Say: **God made water to keep us healthy. He knows we need a lot of water, so he put water in lots of things, like the fresh fruit you ate. Let's see another reason God made water.**

3. Water Cleans Us

Empty one of the bowls of fruit from the previous activity. Point out how dirty the bowl is, and then ask:

● **Why do we need to clean this bowl?**

● **How do you think we can clean this bowl?**

Say: **We need to clean things so we'll stay healthy. If we don't clean this bowl, it could grow germs that make us sick. That's where water comes in really handy. Water is great for making things clean and healthy!** Ask:

● **Do you like to take baths or showers?**

Say: **If we didn't clean ourselves, we wouldn't be very healthy. We might not smell very good, either! Let's do a rhyme with motions to remind us how water keeps us healthy by cleaning us.**

Rain from the sky will wash the trees. (*Wiggle your fingers down as rain.*)

Water from a hose can wash a dog's fleas. (*Scratch your sides.*)

An elephant sprays water from its trunk so high. (*Raise an arm up in front of your nose as a trunk.*)

But right into the tub go I. (*Pretend to wash your arms.*)

To a rain puddle, birds can fly. (*Flap your arms.*)

A swimming goldfish will never be dry. (*Put your hands together and "swim" them.*)

Under a sprinkler a dog can lie. (*"Wag" a hand behind you.*)

But right into the tub go I. (*Pretend to wash your arms.*)

Repeat the rhyme if you have time. Then say: **God wants us to be healthy, so he made water. Water can help us stay clean and can help us clean other things. God is so good to give us water!**

Water Is in the Bible

1. God Waters the Plants

Gather the children together around a table, and set out the cup of seeds and the plant. Ask:

● **How are seeds and plants the same? How are they different?**

Say: **When we plant seeds, they grow into plants. These seeds are plants that are waiting to grow.** Ask:

● **How do you plant seeds?**

● **What do seeds need in order to grow?**

Help children realize that seeds need water to grow into plants.

Open your Bible to Psalm 147:7-8. Say: **Listen to what the Bible says about how God takes care of plants.** Read the Scripture to the children, and ask:

● **How does God help plants to grow?**

● **What happens to plants that don't get any water?**

Say: **Seeds need water to grow into plants, and plants need water to live. God made water so the plants can grow and be healthy. Let's make flowers to show that water makes plants healthy.**

Give each child a paper plate "flower." Spread newspaper on a table, and set out the crayons or markers. Have children color their flowers and then sit in a circle with their flowers.

Say: **We're going to pretend that each one of you is a seed planted in the ground. When the sun comes out and you are watered, you will grow and let your flower bloom. Let's crouch down so we look like seeds.** Show children how to crouch down into a ball, and then say: **Good! Now let's pretend that we're being watered. How do you think a seed would feel when it's being watered?** Allow children to respond. To pretend you're being watered, you could gently pat your head or tickle your neck. Encourage children to do different motions to pretend they're being watered. Then say: **Great! Now let's pretend that we're growing and growing until we're full-grown flowers.** With the children, slowly stretch up higher and higher until your hands are above your head and you're holding your flower up high. Then say: **Now let's do our motions together while I read a story.**

A little boy was walking one day when he found a bag of seeds. He decided to take the seeds home and plant them to see what would

grow. He pushed each seed into the ground and covered it with dirt. *(Crouch down.)* **The sun was shining brightly. The little boy watered the seeds.** *(Pretend you're being watered.)* **The next morning, the sun came out and shone warmly on the seeds. The boy watered his seeds again.** *(Pretend you're being watered.)* **This happened for many days until one day, the little boy saw plants coming out of the ground. During the next few days, the plants slowly grew until they bloomed into beautiful flowers.** *(Slowly stretch up until you're holding your flower above your head.)*

Have the children sit down again, and then ask:
- **Why do you think God made water?**
- **How does water help the plants?**

Say: **God made the water to keep us healthy. God keeps the plants healthy with water, too.**

2. I Am Thirsty

Say: **God helps the plants by sending rain. God wants us to help other people by sharing.** Ask:
- **What does it mean to share with someone? Tell us about a time you shared something with another person.**

Open your Bible to Matthew 10:42 and 25:40, and read the Scripture aloud. Say: **Jesus is telling us that when we share a cup of water with another person who is thirsty, it is as though we are sharing it with him. We're going to play a game in which each of us will get to share a pretend cup of water with someone else.** Have children form a circle. Give the large plastic cup full of blue ribbons to one of the children beside you, and say: **I am thirsty. Will you give me some water?** Have the child say in response, "I love Jesus. Yes, I will." Have the child take a piece of ribbon out of the cup and give it to you. Continue the game until each child has a piece of ribbon. Ask:
- **Why is it important for us to share water with each other?**

Say: **God loves us, so he made water to keep us healthy. We can show love to others by sharing with them the good things God has made.** Have children take home their ribbons to remind them that God gives us water.

3. Well Watchers

Open your Bible to John 4:1-14, and show children the passage. Explain that this is a true story from the Bible.

Say: **When Jesus lived on earth, people didn't have faucets or drinking fountains to get their water from. They had to dig deep holes in the** ground to find water. These holes were called wells. Everyone get your pretend shovel, and help me dig a well. Have children pretend to dig with you.

Wow! We just dug a deep hole. Put several chairs back-to-back in a circle as a well. Let's see what's down there. Have children peer into the well. Look at all the water! Since our well is so deep, how will we get the water out? Let children share their ideas.

When Jesus was on earth, people would drop a container into the well with a rope and then pull it up full of water. Let's use this bucket to get water out of our well. Using one hand, set the bucket in the center of the chairs. People had to go to the well many times so they would have enough water. I will give each one of you a reason to go to the well and pull up the bucket to get some water. Have each child take a turn at the well, making sure to leave the string outside the well for the next person. Give children biblical-time needs such as watering camels or donkeys, washing feet, watering plants, drinking water, cooking with water, and so on.

Say: The Bible tells us that Jesus had to walk a long way from a town called Judea to a town called Galilee. It was so hot and dry, and Jesus was thirsty and tired. He came to a well like our well, and he knew he could find water there. He sat until a woman came to the well to get some water. Then he asked the woman, "Will you give me a drink?" The woman was very surprised because usually people didn't talk to her at the well. Then Jesus told her that he could give her something even better than a drink of water. He could help her live with God in heaven.

Wow! Jesus asked for a drink of water, but he can give us something much better than a drink of water. Jesus can help us live with God in heaven. A drink of water is a very wonderful thing, but living with God is very, very, very wonderful! I bet that woman was glad Jesus asked her for a drink of water.

Let's Thank God for Water

1. Prayer Picture

Have the children sit around the table you covered with newspaper earlier. Set out the crayons, white paper, and stickers.

Say: We're going to thank God for water by making a prayer picture. Give each child a piece of paper. Repeat the words of the prayer after me, and then I will show you what to do on your paper.

Thank you, God, for water that keeps us healthy, clean, and cool.

Have children use crayons to color water on part of their papers.

Thank you, God, for fruit that gives us water to eat. Have the children put fruit stickers on their papers.

Thank you, God, for your love. You made water to keep us healthy because you love us so much. Have children put a heart sticker on their papers.

In Jesus' name, amen.

Let children finish their pictures by drawing their favorite ways to enjoy water—drinking or swimming, for example.

God Created Weather

Preschoolers love to interact with weather. They go out of their way to stomp in rain puddles; they throw leaves into the wind to see how far they fly; and they catch snowflakes on their tongues. Weather is interesting and fun!

Weather is also part of God's grand design for the earth. Rain and snow provide plants and animals with water to drink. Wind carries seeds to new locations. Seasonal changes in temperature cause the land to either produce or rest. Use this lesson to help children learn that our infinitely wise, graciously loving God is indeed the father of our wonderful weather.

Supply List

- a Bible
- a bowl of ice
- a small fan
- a small lamp
- a spray bottle filled with water
- several items of child-sized or adult-sized clothing, such as galoshes, beach shoes, sweaters, raincoats, stocking hats, shorts, scarves, umbrellas, and sunglasses
- crayons
- a "Weather Wheel" handout (p. 90) for each child
- scissors
- glue
- small and large paper plates
- brads
- blue, red, white, and purple streamers
- ½ banana per child
- cream cheese frosting
- several shakers of powdered sugar

Preparation

Near an electrical outlet, set the bowl of ice, fan, spray bottle, and lamp.

Cut out an arrow and a weather wheel from the "Weather Wheel" handout (p. 90) for each child.

God Created Weather

1. All Kinds of Weather

After children have arrived, have them gather around you. Ask:

● **Do you like the weather today? Why or why not?**

● **What different kinds of weather can you think of?**

Say: **God made lots of different kinds of weather.** Pick up the bowl of ice. Say: **God made cold, snowy weather. These ice cubes will help us remember what cold or snowy weather feels like. When it's cold or snowy, animals like bears go to sleep and many plants lose their leaves.** Ask:

● **What do you like to do when it's as snowy or cold as these ice cubes?**

While children respond, pass around the ice for them to touch. Set the bowl of ice out of the children's reach. Then plug in the fan, and set it on the floor. Say: **God made the wind, too. This fan will help us remember what windy weather feels like. When it's windy outside, seeds from plants and flowers blow around so new plants will grow in new places.** Ask:

● **What do you like to do when it's as windy as the wind from this fan?**

While children respond, carefully blow the fan's wind onto each child's face. Be careful not to let the children touch the fan. Set the fan out of the children's reach, plug in the small lamp, and say: **God also made hot weather. This lamp will help us remember what hot weather feels like. When it's hot, plants and flowers grow big and tall.** Ask:

● **What do you like to do when it's as hot as the light from this lamp?**

While children respond, have them place their palms under the light. Set the lamp out of the children's reach, and pick up the spray bottle. Then say: **God also made rain. This spray bottle will help us remember what rainy weather feels like. When it's rainy, plants and animals can get a drink.** Ask:

● **What do you like to do when it's as rainy as the water from this spray bottle?**

While children respond, mist their hands with the spray bottle. Then set the spray bottle out of the children's reach. Ask:

● **Why do you think God made so many different kinds of weather?**

Then say: **God made all the different kinds of weather in the world to keep everything healthy. Now let's play a game that shows one reason we pay attention to the different kinds of weather God made.**

2. What to Wear?

Have the children sit in a circle. Set out the clothing items and accessories you gathered before class. Explain that you'll walk around the circle and say,

"Rain or shine, rain or shine." Then you'll tap a child on the head and name a type of weather—"God made a snowy day!" for example. That child will walk quickly to the pile of clothes, pick out an item he or she would wear for that type of weather, put on that item, and tell why he or she chose that item. Finally, the child will remove the item and return to the circle.

After the children understand the game, play enough rounds for everyone to have a chance to dress up. Encourage children to call out suggestions to the child who's dressing up. After each child has had a chance to dress up, ask:

● **What other decisions does weather help us to make?**

Say: **Sometimes it's hard to know what the weather is going to be like. Then it's hard to know what to wear. Let's make weather wheels to help you remember what to wear in different kinds of weather.**

3. Weather Wheels

Set out crayons, and distribute weather wheels from the "Weather Wheel" handout (p. 90). Ask:

● **What picture shows what we wear on cold days? warm days? windy days? rainy days?**

Allow children to each color a handout and then glue a weather wheel to a paper plate. Use a brad to secure an arrow as a pointer for each weather wheel. Be sure each child's name is on his or her weather wheel.

When everyone has made a weather wheel, say: **Before you go to sleep at night, ask someone to help you figure out what the weather is supposed to be like the next day. Then move your arrow until it points to the right picture. The arrows on your weather wheels say, "God made weather." The Bible talks about the weather. Let's find out more about that.**

Have children set aside their weather wheels.

Weather Is in the Bible

1. God Made It All

Hold up a Bible opened to the book of Job. Say: **The book of Job tells about a man named Job who was very sad. God knew that Job was sad and wanted Job to trust him. Job needed to remember that God is powerful and wise, so God talked to Job about the weather!** Ask:

● **Why do you think weather reminded Job of God's power and wisdom?**

● **How does weather remind you that God is powerful and wise?**

Give blue streamers and red streamers to half of the children; give white

Teacher Tip

You can alter the types of weather in this game by using variations such as drizzly, drippy, frosty, freezing, blustery, or boiling.

streamers and purple streamers to the other half.

Tell the children with the blue streamers that when you mention rain, they should stand up, wave their streamers; and shout, "God made the rain!" Tell the children with the red streamers that when you mention heat, they should stand up, wave their streamers, and shout, "God made the heat!" Tell the children with the white streamers that when you mention snow, they should stand up, wave their streamers, and shout, "God made the snow!" Tell the children with the purple streamers that when you mention wind, they should stand up, wave their streamers, and shout, "God made the wind!"

After children understand, read aloud this adaptation of Job 38:22-30:

To remind Job that God is powerful and wise, God asked, "Job, do you know where I keep the snow and hail?" Have the children with the white streamers respond. **"Do you know where lightning is born? I do! Do you know where the winds begin? I do!"** Have the children with purple streamers respond. **"Who makes the rain and the thunderstorms that give the land water to drink? I do!"** Have the children with blue streamers respond. **"In the desert, where it's very hot and dry, who makes the rain that causes grass to grow? I do!"** Have the children with red streamers and blue streamers respond. **"Who makes the weather so cold that ice and frost and snow form? I do!"** Have the children with white streamers respond. Ask:

● **What kinds of weather did God make?** Have all the children respond together. Collect the streamers to use again some other time, and then ask:

● **What does the weather tell us about God?**

Say: **The weather can remind us that God is wise and powerful.**

2. God Made Storms

Have the children sit in a circle on the floor. Hold up a Bible, and read aloud Zechariah 10:1. Say: **Rainy, stormy weather reminded this person of God. Let's make our own "storm" to help us remember God.**

Have the children practice making the following sounds. Demonstrate each sound for the children, and then have them mimic you.

● Rub your palms back and forth.
● Drum your fingers on the floor.
● Snap your fingers.

- Clap lightly.
- Pound the floor with your fists.
- Clap loudly.

Explain that to make the storm, you'll make a sound, point to a child, and *only* that child will continue to make the sound. Rub your palms together, and point to a child. Then drum your fingers, and point to a child, and so on. Continue until the storm is raging; then reverse the sounds until the storm has dissipated.

Say: **We made a pretend rainstorm, but God makes real rainstorms! Rain and storms can be very gentle, or they can be very powerful. God is gentle, and God is also strong and powerful.**

3. Snowcapped Mountains

Open a Bible to Job 37:6, and show the page to the children. Read aloud the verse, and then say: **This verse tells us that God is in charge of the weather. Today we're going to make a snack called "Snowcapped Mountains" to help us remember that.**

Have the children wash their hands and sit at tables. Cut bananas in half, and have the children peel their bananas and place them on paper plates. Invite the children to dip their bananas in the cream cheese frosting to create snowcapped mountains.

Before children eat their snacks, pass around a shaker or sifter of powdered sugar so children can make it "snow" on their mountains. While everyone eats, ask children what kind of weather is their favorite.

After the snack, say: **God is good because he gives us the weather our world needs. Let's thank God for the weather he made.**

Remind children to throw away their plates and to wash their hands.

Let's Thank God for Weather

1. Weather Prayer Rhyme

Have the children stand in a circle. Say: **We learned today that God made weather. Let's say a fun prayer to thank God for all the different kinds of weather we can think of.** Teach the children the following rhyme, inserting any kind of weather.

> **God, I thank you for this day**
> **And for the** [kind of weather] **you send my way!**

Then have children hold hands, swing their hands back and forth, and each take a turn saying the rhyme. You may need to help by saying the rhyme with the children but allowing each child to say a kind of weather. Have the children close the prayer by jumping up and saying "Amen!"

God made weather +

God Created Wind and Air

God took some nitrogen, a little oxygen, added a bit of carbon dioxide, and created air—that wonderful, invisible substance that saturates the earth and enables all things to live and breathe.

How can we teach preschoolers about something they can't see? We can help them see how it works. In this lesson, preschoolers will feel air move and see it fill bubbles and evaporate water. Then they will "become" the wind as they learn about how God spoke to Elijah. Through these experiences, preschoolers can learn that God is all around us, just as the air is! Set your sails to lead your children in a "winderful" time.

Supply List

- a Bible
- bubble-blowing solution with bubble wand
- small cups
- newspaper
- white paper
- a straw for each child
- watered-down red, yellow, and blue paint
- a large craft stick for each child
- tape
- crepe-paper streamers
- scissors
- an electric fan (with safety features so little fingers can't fit through metal bars)

- lightweight down-type feathers
- spray perfume
- a table tennis ball
- a basket
- three wet paper towels
- four clothespins
- a resealable plastic sandwich bag
- one yard of cord or heavy string
- inexpensive flimsy white paper plates
- a permanent marker
- crayons or markers
- yarn
- a stapler

Teacher Tip

If you don't have bubble blowers, make one for each child from a pipe cleaner. Simply loop one end of the pipe cleaner to make a circle.

Preparation

For each child, place a bubble blower and bubble-blowing solution in a small cup.

Make one sample kite for the "Colorful Kites" activity. (See instructions on p. 92.). Also cut three nine-inch crepe-paper streamers for each child.

Tape several crepe-paper streamers to the bars of the electric fan.

God Created Wind and Air

1. Bubbles Floating in the Air

Gather children around you. Say: **Air is all around us. We can't really see air, but when it moves, we can see what it moves. We call air that moves "wind."**

● **What things have you seen the wind blow?**

● **Can you make wind come out of your mouth and blow on your hand?**

Say: **God created air so all living things could breathe. We're going to use the air in our mouths to do something fun.**

Dip a bubble wand into bubble-blowing solution. Blow a bubble, and catch it on the bubble wand. Then pass out the cups with solution and bubble wands to the children, and let them blow bubbles.

After a few minutes of play, say: **Isn't God wonderful to create air for us to breathe and to play with?**

2. Blow, Paint, Blow

Spread newspaper on a table and the floor, and set out the paper, straws, and paint.

Say: **We need air to live. When we breathe in, we take fresh air into our bodies. When we breathe out, we let old air out of our bodies. Let's take some fresh air in through our noses and then blow it out through our mouths.** Practice inhaling and exhaling with the children.

Say: **God gave us air to breathe, but we can also use it to make bubbles and fly paper airplanes. We can even paint with air!**

Put three small puddles of paint—red, yellow, and blue—on each child's paper. Then demonstrate how to blow the paint with the straw to spread it out.

Have children wash any paint residue from their hands.

3. Colorful Kites

Show the children the sample kite. Ask:

● **Why isn't my kite flying?**

● **How do you think I could get it to fly?**

Say: **The air isn't moving right now. But if we run, we will be running through the air. Then do you think we can get the kite to fly?**

Hold up the kite, and run around the room. Then set out the craft sticks, tape, and crepe-paper streamers. Have the children bunch up one end of each crepe-paper streamer and then line up the three bunched up ends on the top third of a craft stick. Help the children secure their streamers with tape. When the children have finished their kites, let them take the kites outside to fly them.

After a few minutes of play, have the children come back inside. Ask:

- **What made your kites fly?**
- **What other things use wind and air to fly?**
- **Why do you think God made the wind and air?**

Say: **God made air that can hold kites and bubbles.**

Wind and Air Are in the Bible

1. Even the Wind Obeys

Gather children around the electric fan, and set out the Bible, the feathers, perfume, a straw for each child, a table tennis ball, and a basket.

Open your Bible to Mark 4:41, and show the page to the children. Say: **The Bible says that the wind obeys Jesus. If it were a very windy day and I went outside and yelled, "Stop, wind!" would the wind stop for me?** Allow children to respond. **No, it wouldn't. But it would obey Jesus.**

I can make a little wind blow, though, by turning on this fan. Look at what happens to the streamers when the wind moves them. Turn on the fan, and allow the children to come up one at a time to feel the wind on their faces. The streamers will prevent preschoolers from getting too close. Then drop a few feathers in front of the fan, and watch them float. Have the children sit back, away from the fan. Tell the children to stand up as soon as they can smell perfume. Then spray some perfume in front of the fan. When all the children are standing, have them move to a table. Take the straws, basket, and table tennis ball with you.

Say: **We're going to play a game in which you blow wind out of your mouth to move this ball across the table and into a basket.**

Have the children form two groups and line up at opposite ends of the table. Give the first child in one line a basket with which to catch the ball at the end of the table. Give the first child in the other line a straw and the ball to blow to the opposite side of the table. Let children take turns until everyone has had a chance to play. Then ask:

- **How did the ball get from one side of the table to the other?**

Say: **God made the wind and air to move things. We can use air from our mouths to move very small things, but the real wind obeys Jesus.**

2. God's Whisper (from 1 Kings 19:1-13)

Say: **Now let's hear a story from the Bible about wind** (based on 1 Kings 19:1-13). Have the children form a circle. Choose one child to be "Elijah" and stand outside the circle. Explain that children will be the wind, earthquake, fire, and God's whisper. Give each child except Elijah two streamers.

Say: **Long ago, a man named Elijah loved God and told others about him. Elijah was very sad because the people didn't love God. God told Elijah to go to a cave on a mountain because he, the Lord, was about to pass by.** Have Elijah walk around the circle once and then go to the middle of the circle. Say: **Then a great and powerful wind came and broke many rocks on the mountain.** Have the children in the circle hold their streamers over their heads and slowly run around the circle. Say: **But that wind was not the Lord. Then an earthquake came and cracked part of the mountain.** Have the children in the circle face Elijah and stomp up and down in place, alternating their hands up and down over their heads. Say: **But the earthquake was not the Lord. Then a fire came and burned part of the mountain.** Have the children face Elijah and quickly wave their streamers up and down. Say: **But the fire was not the Lord.** Whisper: **Then came a gentle whisper. When Elijah heard the whisper, he went out from the cave and listened to the quiet whisper. God was speaking to Elijah.** Have Elijah stand up and listen. Have the children in the circle put their fingers to their mouths and gently blow on them.

Say: **Blow gently on your finger. That's how gently God whispered to Elijah. God whispers to us, too. Be sure to listen.**

If you have time, allow different children to be Elijah, and play again.

3. God Remembered Noah

Set out three wet paper towels, four clothespins, and the sandwich bag. Tie the cord or string between two chairs as a clothesline. Then set up the fan to blow on the clothesline.

Open your Bible to Genesis 8:1, show the page to the children, and say: **God does so many things with wind and air. The Bible says God can dry up water with wind and air. We're going to hang out three paper towels in three different ways to see which one the air dries the fastest.** Hang up the first paper towel like a sheet. Fold the second paper towel three times before hanging it. Then put the third paper towel into the bag, and hang the bag on the line. Ask:

● **Which towel can the air blow best?**

● **Which paper towel do you think will dry fastest? Why?**

Turn on the fan; then go to the next activity. After that activity, have the children touch the paper towels. Then say: **Aren't you glad God made air to dry things out?**

Let's Thank God for Wind and Air

1. Air Mail Prayers to Jesus

Say: **Today we're going to pretend to be prayers floating through the air up to Jesus. Each of you will get a paper streamer to hold as you gently twirl around the room repeating the prayers I say to Jesus.**

Distribute streamers; then have children repeat these lines after you:

Thank you, God, for the air we breathe.

Thank you, God, for air that dries things.

Thank you, God, for the air that's inside bubbles.

Thank you, God, for the air that helps kites fly.

Thank you, God, for air that moves and tickles our faces.

Thank you, God, for giving us air.

Bible Story Index

Scripture Index